UNDERUTILIZED FOOD FOR PREGNANT WOMEN

By

Ankita Saxena

Lecturer
Major S.D. Singh Mahila P.G. College
Mohmmadabad
Farrukhabad

Dr. Amita Jain

State Programme Representative
Micronutrient Initiatives
(U.P.)

&

Dr. Amita Jain

Officer Incharge
Deptt. of Extension
Communication Management
Faculty of Home Science
C.S. Azad University of
Agriculture & Technology
Kanpur (U.P.)

DISCOVERY PUBLISHING HOUSE PVT. LTD.

NEW DELHI-110 002

Published by:
Tilak Wasan

DISCOVERY PUBLISHING HOUSE PVT. LTD.
4831/24, Prahlad Street, Ansari Road
Darya Ganj, New Delhi-110002 (India)
Phone : +91-11-23279245, 43764432
Fax : +91-11-23253475
E-mail : parul.wasan@gmail.com
discoverypublishinghouse@gmail.com
info@discoverypublishinggroup.com
web : www.discoverypublishinggroup.com

***First Edition:* 2011**
ISBN: 978-81-8356-717-6

Underutilized Food for Pregnant Women

Printed at:
Shree Balaji Art Press
Delhi

Dedicated
To
My Beloved Parents
Who
Signify
The Very
Existence of Me

Preface

Maternal nutrition plays a role in certain types of fetal malformations or spontaneous abortion. Because these abnormalities occur so early in pregnancy modifications must be made before pregnancy begins. A women whose diet in adequate before pregnancy is usually able to bear a full term viable infant, without extensive modifications of her diet. Mother's diet should produce adequate nutrients so that maternal stores do not get depleted and produce sufficient milk to nourish her child after birth. The nutritional demands are highly increased in an adolescent mother.

The nutritional needs of a pregnant are always higher than that of a pregnant women. As far as nutrition for healthy pregnancy is variety of nutritional items in her diet. This is needed for getting the amount of calories, vitamins, carbohydrates and protein recommended by the physician.

A pregnant women needs extra care and good nutrition for both himself and the foetus developing in her womb. As far as the nutrition in concerned, mother should develop healthy nutritional habits. Proper intake of nutrients is necessary for healthy pregnancy.

This book focus on the effect of nutrition on pregnant women, diet for pregnant women and physiological changes during pregnancy.

Ankita Saxena
Amita Jain
Neelma Kunwar

Acknowledgements

In this perishable world there are still a few things, which are imperishable. One of them is knowledge, not easy till one gets a mentor. It is my proud privilege and great opportunity to work under such inspiring guidance and constructive criticism of *Dr. Amita Jain*, State Programme Representative, Micronutrient Initiatives, Uttar Pradesh. Her untiring supervision, persistent encouragement, unending zeal and conspicuous ability has always been a constant source of my achievement. I am extremely indebted to her for being meticulous throughout our investigation and preparation of this manuscript.

I also bestow my heartful thanks gratitude to *Dr. Pratibha Arya* and *Dr. Minakshi Singh*, Lecturer, HDFS, Institute of Home Science, Bundelkhand University, Jhansi for their timely guidance and creative suggestions during the tenure of the present study.

From the inner core of my heart, uncountable words of cordial veneration and gratitude are dedicated to the pious feet of my father *Sri Ram Gopal Saxena* and my mother *Smt Shanti Devi Saxena* for their love, affection, good wishes, blessings, constant encouragement and inspiration showed by them for the achievement of my present educational asset. I also express my warm appreciation to my brother-in-law *Sri Satyendra Kumar Sinha*, my sisters *Smt Anamica Sinha* and *Poonam, Lucky* and loving brothers *Rahul* and *Sumit* who extended moral support, timely help and constant inspiration to me during the entire period of my study.

It was difficult task for me to find appropriate words and express my sincere appreciation to my friends *Mintu*

Mohammad Akil, Dr *Mani Mishra, Garima* and all my sisters who helped me a lot during my research work.

Many more people who helped me directly or indirectly during course of studies, if I don't list them all, its not for lack of gratitude, it is lack of space. To them all, I convey my best compliments and lot of thanks.

With the blessing of almighty 'God', I am presenting this research work.

Ankita Saxena

Contents

1

CHAPTER

Introduction

Pregnancy is optimal when the mother is biologically mature. A biologically mature female is a young woman who is at least 5 years post menarcheal and this has greater impact on pregnancy than her chronological age.

Pregnancy is a critical period in women's life cycle, it is a period of increased metabolic demands with changes in the women's physiology and the requirement of growing foetus.

Adequate nutrition before and during pregnancy has greater potential for a long term health impact than it does at any other time. Maternal health is complex, influenced by various genetic, social and economic factors, infections and environmental conditions, many of which may affect the foetal growth. Physiological adaptations result in improved utilization of nutrients either through increased absorption, decreased excretion or alternations in metabolism.

A woman who has been well nourished before conception begins her pregnancy with reserves of several nutrients so that the needs of the growing foetus can be met without affecting her health. Infants, who are well nourished in the womb, have an enhanced chance of entering life in good physical and mental health. The effects of under nutrition during reproduction will vary depending upon the nutrients involved, the length of time it is lacking and the stage of gestation at which it occurs.

A woman whose diet is adequate before pregnancy is usually able to bear a full term viable infant, without extensive modifications of her diet. Mother's diet should produce adequate nutrients so that maternal stores do not get depleted and produce sufficient milk to nourish her child after birth. The nutritional demands are highly increased in an adolescent mother.

PHYSIOLOGICAL CHANCES OF PREGNANCY

The expansion of blood volume is required to allow the circulation of blood through the placenta and allow it carry nutrients and oxygen to the foetus and metabolic wastes away from the foetus. Blood volume expands by 50 per cent resulting in a decrease in haemoglobin levels, blood glucose values and serum levels of albumin, other serum proteins and water-soluble vitamins. The decline in serum albumin level contributes to a tendency for extra cellular water to accumulate during pregnancy. The decrease in water soluble vitamin concentration makes determination of an inadequate intake or a deficient nutrient state difficult. By contrast, serum concentrations of fat soluble vitamins and other lipid fractions, such as triglycerides, cholesterol and free fatty acids increase.

There is a decreased ability to taste saltiness. This may in fact, be a physiologic mechanism for increasing salt intake. Increased progesterone level relaxes the uterine muscle to allow expansion with fetal growth. Gastrointestinal motility diminishes, to allow for increased absorption of nutrients. This often results in constipation. Additionally, a relaxed lower oesophageal sphincter can cause regurgitation and heart burns.

Increased blood volume produces a high glomerular filtration rate. It appears that the renal tubules are unable to adjust completely and a percentage of nutrients that would have been reabsorbed in the non-pregnant women are excreted in the urine. Increased amounts of amino acids, glucose and water soluble vitamins may appear in the urine. This may be a reason for the increased number of urinary tract infections seen in pregnant women.

The ability to excrete water is lowered and oedema in the legs and ankles is common and normal.

Less than half of the total weight gain resides in the foetus, placenta and amniotic fluid; the remainder is found in maternal reproductive tissues, fluid, blood and maternal stores, a component composed largely of body fat. Gradually increasing subcutaneous fat in the abdomen, back and upper thigh serves as an energy reserve for pregnancy and lactation.

Increased weight gain during pregnancy is associated with increased birth weight and a progressive decrease in the number of LBW infants. High oestrogen levels during pregnancy promote a gynicoid type of fat distribution.

Role of Placenta

The placenta is the principal site of production for several hormones responsible for regulation of fetal growth and development of maternal support tissues. It is also involved for exchange of nutrients, oxygen and waste products. Any damage to or inadequacy in the placenta compromises its ability to nourish the foetus, regardless of how well nourished the mother is or how optimal her dietary intake.

Preconceptual Nutrition

Maternal nutrition plays a role in certain types of fetal malformations or spontaneous abortion. Because these abnormalities occur so early in pregnancy (during organogenesis) modifications must be made before pregnancy begins. In diabetes, incidence of congenital defects can be reduced almost to normal by bringing the blood glucose under good control prior to pregnancy. Administration of folic acid 400-800 mcg per day around and during conception and early gestation can reduce the incidence of neural tube defects. In addition, women with low body weight and poor nutritional status prior to pregnancy have more low birth weight infants, premature spontaneous rupture of membranes, infection and anaemia.

On the other end of the spectrum, overweight women are more likely to have fetal death, diabetes, hypertensive disorders and labour abnormalities. Because these maladies are difficult to correct once pregnancy begins, a woman should achieve a body mass within 90–120 per cent of ideal weight prior to conception. Due to undernourishment of the mother the baby is at an increased risk of being premature with low birth weight and developmental irregularities. Intrauterine nutrition is highly important for the growth of the central nervous system and kidneys of the foetus which mature during the later part of pregnancy. Therefore nutrition deficits before birth can never be wholly reversed after birth.

NUTRITIONAL REQUIREMENTS OF PREGNANCY

Increase in nutritional requirements depend on the nature of metabolic changes of pregnancy and the nutrition reserves of the mother. Malnutrition is an ecological problem and affects every stage of life span. Globally around 6,00,000 women die every year from pregnancy related causes and many of them were short, thin, and anaemic and have a variety of micro nutrient deficiency. In developing country, Indian women are frequently malnourished and often have a poor pregnancy out-come.

There are many myths surrounding the diet for pregnant mothers. We often hear the elders of the family advising young mothers to eat enough for two individuals. Today, we know that this is not true. In fact, unbridled eating during pregnancy can make one put on a lot of weight and can make her child unnecessarily overweight. What then could be the best diet for pregnant women?

The growing foetus derives all its nourishment from its mother through the umbilical cord. Therefore, while the mother does not have to eat enough food for two individuals, it is important that she take enough nutrients for two individuals. If the mother suffers from nutrient deficiency, this will be passed on to the child. Early nutrient deficiency can lead to a number of developmental problems in young children.

The pregnancy diet must be rich in all the vital nutrients that the body needs. Doctors recommend the intake of six to seven servings of bread and grains, two to four servings of fruit, four to six servings of vegetables, two to four servings of dairy and approximately three servings of protein every day. It is always advisable to choose food that is rich in fiber. Excellent examples include whole-grain cereals, rice, fruits and fresh green veggies.

Calcium is vital for the growth of bones and teeth. It is important to take in at least four servings of calcium rich dairy products. This will ensure that one get approximately 1200 mg of calcium every day. The diet of pregnant women should be rich in iron.

Vitamin C helps strengthen the immune system of the mother and child. Important sources of vitamin C include citrus fruits, broccoli, cauliflower, papaya, green peppers and tomatoes. Vitamin A is equally important. Carrots, sweet potatoes, spinach, turnip, apricots and water squash contain lots of vitamin A.

An expectant mother must always take all the prescribed prenatal vitamins. These are specially devised multivitamins that compensate for any nutrient imbalances or deficiencies in the mother's diet. Generally, these contain iron, minerals, vitamins, folic acid and calcium. The deficiency of folic acid can lead to serious birth defect in babies. Green leafy vegetables, nuts, citrus fruits and beans are rich in natural folic acid, vitamins and iron.

Just as there are things that must be included in the diet for pregnant women, there are certain items that must be avoided during pregnancy. This includes alcohol, caffeine, surplus sugar, surplus fat and raw meat. It is advisable to avoid soft cheese, and to abstain from eating shark, swordfish and mackerel which high levels of mercury in them.

Most pregnant mothers feel nausea and depressing lack of appetite during their first trimester. At this stage, they may eat small meals throughout the day.

Many women put on a lot of weight due to the high fat, salt and sugar content in their pregnancy diet. It is true that pregnant women often go through strong cravings and sharp hunger pangs. But if you desire to keep your weight under control and shed extra pounds quickly after delivery, then, it is important to eat foods low in calories and high in nutritive value.

Diet for Pregnant Woman

Pregnancy planet is the only community on the web dedicated to pregnant and TTC parents. We provide week by week pregnancy information, symptoms and advice along with parenting tips and solutions, conception due date calculator, celebrity baby news, free TTC tickets and blinkies and much more.

Nutrition for Pregnancy Women

Indian women need to maintain a high quality diet during their pregnancy. The baby inside depends on the mother for nutrition. During pregnancy, a mother while maintaining a balanced and nutritious diet, must also focus on key supplemental nutrients that are important for the baby's health. Here are some tips that will help.

- Pregnancy diet – Recommended Dietary Allowances
- Foods rich in protein
- Foods rich in calcium
- Foods rich in iron
- Foods rich in folic acid
- Foods rich vitamin A
- Foods rich in vitamin B_1
- Foods rich in vitamin B_2
- Foods rich in vitamin B_3
- Foods rich in vitamin C
- Iodine

A pregnant woman needs extra care and good nutrition for both herself and the foetus developing in her womb. As far as the nutrition in concerned, mother should develop healthy nutritional habits. Proper intake of nutrients is necessary for healthy pregnancy.

Pregnancy and Nutrition

The nutritional needs of a pregnant are always higher than that of a non-pregnant woman. As far as nutrition for healthy pregnancy is variety of nutritional items in her diet. This is needed for getting the amount of calories, vitamins, carbohydrates and proteins recommended by the physician.

There are many myths surrounding the diet for pregnant mothers. We often hear the elders of the family advising young mothers to eat enough for two individuals. Today, we know that this is not true. In fact, unbridled eating during pregnancy can make one put on a lot of weight and can make her child unnecessarily overweight. What then could be the best diet for pregnant women?

The growing foetus derives all its nourishment from its mother through the umbilical cord. Therefore, while the mother does not have to eat enough food for two individuals, it is important that she take is passed on to the child. Early nutrient deficiency can lead to a number of developmental problems in young children.

The pregnancy diet must be rich in all the vital nutrients that the body needs. Doctors recommended the intake of six to seven servings of breads and grains, two to four servings of fruit, four to six servings of vegetables, two to four servings of dairy and approximately three servings of protein every day. It is always advisable to choose food that is rich in fiber. Excellent examples include whole grain cereals, rice, fruits and fresh green veggies.

Calcium is vital for the growth of bones and teeth. It is important to take in at least four servings of calcium rich dairy products. This will ensure that you get approximately 1200 mg of calcium every day. The diet of pregnant women should be rich in iron.

Vitamin C helps strengthen the immune system of the mother and child. Important sources of vitamin C include citrus fruits, broccoli, cauliflower, papaya, green peppers and tomatoes. Vitamin A is equally important. Carrots, sweet potatoes, spinach, turnip apricots and water squash contain lots of vitamin A.

An expectant mother must always take all the prescribed prenatal vitamins. These are specially devised multivitamins that compensate for any nutrient imbalances or deficiencies in the mother's diet. Generally, these contain iron, minerals, vitamins, folic acid and calcium. The deficiency of folic acid can lead to serious birth defect in babies. Green leafy vegetables, nuts, citrus fruits and beans are rich in natural folic acid, vitamins and iron.

Just as there are things that must be included in the diet for pregnant women, there are certain items that must be avoided during pregnancy. These include alcohol, caffeine, surplus sugar, surplus fat and raw meat. It is advisable to avoid soft cheese, and to abstain from eating shark, swordfish and mackerel which high levels of mercury in them.

Most pregnant mothers feel nausea and a depressing lack of appetite during their first trimester. At this stage, they may eat small meals throughout the day.

Many women put on a lot of weight due to the high fat, salt and sugar content in their pregnancy diet. It is true that pregnant women often go through strong cravings and sharp hunger pangs. But if you desire to keep your weight under control and shed extra pounds quickly after delivery, then, it is important to eat foods low in calories and high in nutritive value.

Energy

Energy needs during pregnancy increases because additional energy is required for the following :

- The growth and physical activity of the foetus
- The growth of the placenta
- The normal increase in maternal body size.
- The additional work involved in carrying the weight of the foetus and extra maternal tissues.
- The slow but steady rise in basal metabolic rate during pregnancy.
- Any decrease in the activity of the mother decreases the caloric requirement.

For an Indian woman of 55 kg, the total energy cost of pregnancy is about 80,000 kcals. Of this about 36,000 kcals is deposited as fat, which is utilized subsequently during lactation.

Hence, ICMR recommended energy requirement of pregnant woman is as follows :

Sedentary worker	-	1875 + 300 = 2175
Moderate worker	-	2225 + 300 = 2525
Heavy worker	-	2925 + 300 = 3225

The caloric requirements of a pregnant woman is mostly increased in the latter half of pregnancy. The increase in calories for trimester wise is as follows :

1st trimester	-	10 cals/day
2nd trimester	-	90 cals/day
3rd trimester	-	200 cals/day

Any decrease in the activity of the mother decreases the caloric requirement. It is very evident that normal pregnancy calls for a considerable weight gain over and above that represented by the size of foetus. The fat that accumulates throughout pregnancy (specially for the first 30 weeks) acts as an energy reserve. When the supply of calories are inadequate the fat may be used up to provide the high energy needs of the rapidly growing foetus and to spare the proteins for tissue growth. This results in an increase in the ketones in the urine during the 1st trimester of pregnancy. The foetus does not accumulate any fat except in the cell walls and system. All the fat is synthesized from glucose except for the only essential fatty acid (linoleic acid) which is transferred from the mother to the child.

Protein

The normal protein requirement of an adult woman is 50 g/day. ICMR prescribed for a pregnant woman 65 g/day. Additional protein is essential for :

- rapid growth of the foetus;
- the enlargement of the uterus, mammary glands and placenta;
- increase in maternal circulating blood volume and subsequent demand of increased plasma protein to maintain colloidal osmotic pressure and circulation of tissue fluids;
- formation of amniotic fluid and storage reserves for labour, delivery and lactation;
- the transfer of amino acids from the mother to foetus (up to 20 weeks all amino acids must be provided to

the foetus as it cannot oxidize amino acids as a source of energy).

Protein requirement during pregnancy has been computed on the basis of N accretion. Based on the body weight gain of 12 kg in a normal healthy well nourished pregnant woman, the daily N deposited during the three trimesters is estimated to be 0.1, 0.5 and 0.9 g respectively. After increasing by 50 per cent of convert the factorial value into physiological value for N accretion, and 25 per cent for individual variation, the safe level of intake in terms of a high quality protein during the three trimesters will be 1.2, 6.0, 10.5 g respectively. After adjusting for the dietary protein quality of NPU 65, the safe intake during the latter half of pregnancy recommended by the Nutrition Expert Committee is 15 g/day.

If protein requirements are not met during pregnancy :

- there is increased risk of pregnancy;
- the foetus may grow at the expense of mother;
- maximum growth of the baby cannot be obtained;
- number of cells in tissues particularly in brain may be less.

Protein and calorie deficiency during gestation may result in poor utilization of food by off spring after birth and a failure to ever compensate for early food deprivation. When amino acids are transferred, some big protein molecules also cross the placental barrier which give immunity to the infants. In the total weight gain during pregnancy there is one kg of protein half of which is foetal tissue.

Milk, meat, egg and cheese are complete proteins and of high biological value. Additional protein may be obtained from legumes and whole grains, nuts and oilseeds.

Linoleic Acid

The requirements of linoleic acid during pregnancy is 4–4.5 en%. If invisible fat is 12.5 en% to meet EFA, visible fat is to be 30 g/day.

Calcium

ICMR calcium requirement of adult woman is 400 mg/day. Requirement increases during pregnancy to 1000 mg/day.

Although the infant bones are poorly calcified at the time of birth an appreciable amount of calcium is involved in foetal development. A full term foetal body is made up of 30 g of calcium.

Increased intake of calcium by the mother is highly essential, not only for the calcification of foetal bones and teeth but also for protection of calcium resources of the mother to meet the high demands during lactation.

Two-thirds of foetal calcium is transferred from the mother to the foetus after 30th week of pregnancy at the rate of 300 mg per day. Radio isotopic studies revealed that nearly 80 per cent calcium of the foetal skeleton and mother were obtained from the mother's diet, and the rest was obtained from maternal reserves. Pregnant woman usually absorb not less than 40 per cent of the calcium available in their diet. Calcium retention by pregnant woman is of 2 to 5 times the amount needed by the foetus in the 6th and 7th months of pregnancy indicating that maternal reserves are being built up at this stage. The amount of dietary calcium needed is reduced when vitamin D is available. Use of vitamin D and calcium reduces muscular cramps of pregnancy. To prevent 'osteomalacia' mother's diet should contain less of phytic acid, adequate amounts of vitamin D and sufficient amount of calcium. Mothers should avoid repeated pregnancies. Dairy products are a primary source of calcium. Green leafy vegetables also contribute to calcium.

Iron

Normal iron requirement of an adult woman is 30 mg/day. ICMR requirements during pregnancy is 38 mg/day.

The increase in iron by 8 mg/day can be attributed to the following :

- Infants are generally born with high Hb levels of 18-22 g/100 ml of blood. Iron stores in the liver of the infants lasts from 3 to 6 months. Iron is also required for growth of foetus and placenta. To achieve these levels mother must transfer 240 mg of iron to the foetus during gestating.
- It is also required for the formation of haemoglobin as there is 40-50 per cent increased maternal blood volume. For this 400 mg of iron is required.
- Loss of maternal iron through skin and sweat is about 170 mg of iron.

The total iron requirement for the entire period of pregnancy is 810 mg.

The actual increase in requirement of iron is only in second and third trimester. But a single large dose of iron at the beginning of pregnancy is an effective way to build up iron stores and to protect against depletion of reserves. To avoid iron deficiency a woman should enter pregnancy with a store of at least 300 mg of iron.

Liver, dried beans, dried fruits, green leafy vegetables, eggs, enriched cereals and iron fortified salt provide additional sources of iron.

Sodium

Normal adult woman's requirement of sodium should be maintained to prevent any defective disorders and deficiency,

1. During pregnancy there is an increase in the extra cellular fluid which calls for an 80 per cent increase in the body sodium. Restriction in the diet can cause a severe hormonal and biochemical changes.
2. When blood sodium level drops, kidney produces the hormone rennin, as a result of which the sodium that is needed for use by the body is retained.
3. When the system is over taxed it can result in sodium deficiency causing an increased risk of eclampsia, prematurity and low birth weight of infants.

Uses of diuretics should be discouraged during pregnancy as they can cause loss of sodium. Sodium is restricted when there is oedema or hypertension.

Iodine

ICMR recommends additional requirement of 25 μg during pregnancy to the adult requirement of 100-200 μg. Iodine deficiency in mother can lead to abortion, still births, congenital anomalies, increased prenatal mortality, cretinism and psychomotor defects. Mothers who are residing in goiter endemic areas should ensure that they get enough iodine through iodised salt and other means.

Zinc

Zinc deficiency during the antenatal period leads to adverse effects on the newborn including foetal mortality, foetal malformations including—CNS teratogenecity and reduced intra uterine growth rate. Low zinc during pregnancy doubles the risk of low birth weight and trebles the risk of preterm delivery.

Vitamin A

Normal requirements of β carotene for an adult woman is 2400 mcg. Same level is suggested during pregnancy have been calculated on the basis of the vitamin content of livers of the newborn. Additional intake of vitamin A required for this purpose is about 75 μg/day throughout pregnancy. Since this constitutes a small fraction of the recommended allowance for normal women, no additional dietary allowance during pregnancy is suggested. Liver, egg yolk, butter, dark green and yellow vegetables and fruits are good source of vitamin A.

According to studies conducted at National Institute of Nutrition, Hyderabad (1985) that pregnant women of the low income groups have poor vitamin A status as judged by serum vitamin A levels. A daily supplementation of 6000 I.U. for about 12 weeks appears to improve serum vitamin A levels and correct vitamin A deficiency in these pregnant women. Improving vitamin A status of pregnant women reduces maternal mortality.

Excess vitamin A should not be taken during pregnancy.

Vitamin D

Vitamin D is highly essential as it enhances the maternal calcium absorption. Its active form calcidiol and calcitriol cross the placenta with ease and play an important role in calcium metabolism of the foetus. Maternal deficiency of vitamin D results in neonatal hypocalcaemia and hypoplasia. Excessive vitamin D can also result in complications such as atherosclerosis, hypercalcaemia, calcium deposits in various vital organs and mental retardation in the infants.

Vitamin E

In animals vitamin E has an important role to play in the reproductive process and reduces the number of spontaneous abortions and still births. In women it has not been evidently proved that vitamin E deficiency can cause pregnancy failure although they may prove beneficial to those who have had repeated spontaneous abortion or failure to conceive. Very little vitamin E crosses the placenta, so infant has low tissue concentrations that persist up to at least 6 years. Requirement of vitamin E increases with increased intake of PUFA.

Vitamin K

Vitamin K is essential for synthesis of prothrombin that is necessary for normal coagulation of blood. It is highly essential for preventing neonatal haemorrhage. An oral dosage of menadione (synthetic form of vitamin K) during the last weeks of pregnancy or an injection during labour is essential to stimulate prothrombin synthesis. But care should be taken to see that the dosage is given at average level of prevent adverse effects.

Water Soluble Vitamins

Because little of water soluble vitamins are stored, the pregnant woman must rely on her daily intakes that is high enough to meet the added requirements of pregnancy. Generally maternal blood levels for water soluble vitamins tend to fall and foetal blood levels tend to exceed those of mother by 50 to 100 per cent during pregnancy.

Thiamin

ICMR recommendations of thiamin RDA for an adult woman is

0.9 mg for sedentary worker

1.1 mg for moderate worker

1.2 mg for heavy worker

For a pregnant woman the requirement is increased by 0.2 mg/day.

The relationship between thiamin and caloric intake remains the same during pregnancy i.e. for 1000 calories 0.5 mg of thiamin are required. The normal urinary excretion of thiamine drops indicating that more is being retained and used by tissues. In some cases thiamin helps to relieve the nausea of pregnancy.

Riboflavin

ICMR recommendations of riboflavin RDA for an adult woman is :

1.1 mg for sedentary worker

1.3 mg for moderate worker

1.5 mg for heavy worker

In a pregnant woman the RDA is increased by 0.2 mg/day.

Requirements are increased due to increase in maternal body size and growth of foetus and accessory tissues. Riboflavin is present in higher amounts in the foetal blood than in maternal blood. Animal studies have shown that the lack of riboflavin interfere with cartilage formation resulting in skeletal malformations such as shortening of long bones and fusion of ribs.

Niacin

ICMR recommendations of niacin RDA for an adult woman is 12 mg for sedentary worker, 14 mg for moderate worker and 16 mg for heavy worker. In a pregnant woman the RDA is increased by 2 mg, corresponding to the increase in calories. The conversion of amino acid into niacin is more efficient during pregnancy.

Vitamin B_6

Normal requirement of pyridoxine in an adult woman is 2.0 mg. ICMR suggested for pregnancy 2.5 mg/day. In hypertrophy, when the cells are growing in size, B_6 and amino acids are required. During 'toxaemia of pregnancy', (high B.P., oedema, proteinuria) the B_6 levels are lower. Women who used oral contraceptives prior to conception often enter pregnancy with low tissue levels of vitamin B_6. There is no satisfactory theory to explain that these low levels affect the outcome of pregnancy but they do reduce the amount of pyridoxine in breast milk during lactation. B_6 is said to be used to control nausea of pregnancy.

Folic Acid

Normal adult woman requirement of folic acid is 100 µg/day. ICMR recommendations during pregnancy are 400 µg/day. The recommended intake of folacin is based on its role in promoting normal foetal growth and preventing macrocytic anaemia of pregnancy. Folic acid is needed for the synthesis of essential components of DNA and RNA which increase rapidly during growth thereby increasing the requirements. Also folacin is essential for the development of RBCs which must increase as the mothers blood volume increases.

Malformaitons have been noted in the offspring of women using folate antagonist drugs such as methotrexate and valproic acid. There is some evidence in humans to suggest that deficiency of folic acid may be associated with spontaneous abortion and abstetric complications such as preterm labour and low birth weight.

The greatest significance of folic acid and its potential influence on pregnancy outcome is its role in preventing neural tube defects, such as spina bifida. In this condition there is a congenital defect in which the vertebral neural arches fail to close, so exposing the contents of the splinal canal posteriorly. Folic acid deficiency can lead to anencephaly—absence of brain. Folic acid deficiency has also been implicated in pregnancy induced hypertension.

Studies have shown that folic acid acts through an unusual mechanism—terathanasia—the selective promotion of spontaneous abortion of defective foetuses.

All women of childbearing years should take folic acid supplementation. It is crucial to note that, because the neural tube closes by 28 days of gestation (before most women realize that they are pregnant) supplementation with folic acid should ideally occur prior to conception.

Women of childbearing age should be encouraged to include generous amounts of folic acid and sources in their diets—foods such as dark green leafy vegetables, legumes, orange juice, soya, wheat germ, almonds and peanuts. In addition women planning pregnancy should begin periconceptional supplementation with folic acid at levels of 400 to 800 μg/day.

Vitamin B_{12}

Normal adult woman's requirement of vitamin B_{12} is 1 mcg and this requirement remains the same even during pregnancy. The foetus has priority over the mother in B_{12}, and foetal blood has twice the amount of B_{12} than does maternal blood, even when maternal levels are depleted. Low maternal levels are associated with prematurity. The capacity of a woman to absorb B_{12} is increased during pregnancy and a large amount is transferred to the foetus. Vegetarian mothers have more chances of getting B_{12} deficiency. Serum levels drop during pregnancy and return to normal without supplementation after delivery. On the basis of the B_{12} content of foetuses, it has been estimated that foetal demands may be of the order of 0.3 µg/day.

Vitamin C

ICMR recommendations of vitamin C during pregnancy is 40 mg same as normal woman requirement. The foetal requirement is too small and sufficient safety margin is given for an adult women and extra allowance may not be necessary during pregnancy. In pregnancy vitamin C can fully cross the placental barrier. The vitamin C content of foetal blood is thrice as much as maternal blood. There is some evidence to show that the placenta can synthesize vitamin C. This may account for higher levels in foetal tissue. Low maternal intake of vitamin C is associated with premature rupture of foetal membranes and increased neonatal death rates.

A few studies have suggested an association between low plasma levels of vitamin C and preeclampsia.

DIETARY MODIFICATION

For a pregnant woman whose diet has conformed to the 'Basic Five Food' pattern, is merely a matter of emphasizing the more nutrient dense foods within each of the five food groups. Nutrient dense foods are those that give the most nutrients per calorie consumed. Most mothers are concerned enough about the health of their offspring and have a high motivation to eat right food. Pregnancy is perhaps the most effective time to attempt nutrition education.

Usually a daily diet containing 3 cups of milk or its equivalent, 2 servings of meat, fish, poultry eggs, or a source of complete protein, a dark green or yellow vegetables and a generous serving of citrus fruits will provide a foundation for a nutritionally adequate diet. Between the 6th to 14th week of pregnancy 75 per cent women suffer from nausea which in turn affects their appetite. The consumption of small and frequent meals at regular intervals are helpful to many women. This pattern is also very helpful in the later part of pregnancy when discomfort is experienced after large meals due to over crowding by foetus in the abdominal cavity.

Eating a small meal just before hunger sensations usually become most severe, has been a useful method of controlling total intake. Intake must be maintained at steady levels so that the weight gain is not more than 400 g/week, in the 2nd and 3rd trimesters of pregnancy. An erratic weight gain during pregnancy is associated with toxaemia and prematurity.

The selection of diet is also quite complicated because many women experience strong food dislikes and cravings. They often crave for foods they do not take ordinarily and develop strong distastes for foods they previously liked. The certain cases the aroma or sight (ads) to certain foods may evoke strong reactions. Mostly dislikes are oriented towards food that have no nutritional consequences. But if the dislike is for foods such as milk, which has good amounts of calcium then attention should be directed towards such an issue.

Plenty of water at least four to six glasses in addition to what is contained in the form of milk and other beverages should be taken daily throughout pregnancy. This will help keep the bowels regular. It has been found that infection of the tube connecting the kidney and bladder is less common among pregnant women who drink a lot of water. It is recommended that pregnant women limit their intake to 2 cups of caffeine containing beverages per day.

Faulty beliefs and wrong food habits need to be corrected during pregnancy.

GENERAL DIETARY PROBLEMS

Nausea and Vomiting

Nausea in pregnancy may be due to nervous disturbances, placental protein intoxication or due to derangement in carbohydrate metabolism.

Morning sickness of early pregnancy can be improved by small and frequent meals. Fairly dry and consisting chiefly of easily digested energy foods such as carbohydrates are more readily tolerated. Liquids may best be taken between meals instead of with food. If the condition develops to hyperemesis gravidarum, a severe prolonged persistent vomiting, peripheral parenteral nutrition and careful oral feeding is essential. Skim milk is better tolerated than whole milk. Fruits and vegetables can be given. Fatty rich foods, fried foods, excessive seasoning, coffee in large amounts and strongly flavoured vegetables may be restricted or eliminated if the nausea persists or if the patient complains of heartburn or gastric distress.

Constipation

The pressure of the enlarging uterus on the lower portion of the intestine, a addition to the hormonal muscle relaxant effect of placental hormones on the gastrointestinal tract and physical inactivity may make elimination difficult. Increased fluid intake and use of naturally laxative foods such as whole grains, dried fruits and other fruits, vegetables rich fibre, juices usually induce regularity, Laxatives should be avoided. Regular habits of exercise and sleep are essential for proper elimination.

Oedema and Leg Cramps

Mild, physiologic oedema is usually present in the extremities in the third trimester. The swelling of the lower extremities may be caused by the pressure of the enlarging uterus on the veins returning fluid from the legs. This normal oedema requires no sodium restriction or other dietary changes.

The common occurrence of cramps during pregnancy, manifested nocturnally by sudden contractions of the muscle, is thought to be related to a decline in serum calcium levels related to a calcium phosphorus imbalance. Prevention or relief of these leg cramps has been reported with reduction of milk (a high phosphorus, high calcium beverage) intake and supplementation with non-phosphate calcium salts. Magnesium is another mineral with the potential for relieving leg cramps.

Heartburn

Heartburn is a common complaint during the latter part of pregnancy. In most cases, this is an effect of pressure of the enlarged uterus on the stomach which in combination with the relaxation of the oesophageal sphincter, results in occasional regurgitation of the stomach contents into the esophagus. This can usually be relieved by limiting the amount of food consumed at one time and drinking fluids between meals. Sitting upright after meals for at least 3 hours before lying down may also help.

Beliefs Avoidances, Cravings and Aversions

Food avoidances reflect mother's conscious choice not to consume certain foods during pregnancy e.g., heat producing foods like papaya and gingelly seeds.

Cravings and aversions are powerful urges toward or away from foods which women experience no unusual attitudes when not pregnant. The most commonly craved foods are sweets and dairy products. The most common aversions reported are to alcohol, coffee, other caffeinated drinks, meats and strongly spiced foods.

Consumption of non-food items like laundry starch, ice cubes or clay is called pica. It occurs more often during pregnancy than at any other time. The etiology of pica is poorly understood. One theory suggests that the ingestion of non-food substances relieves nausea and vomiting. It has also been hypothesized that a deficiency for essential nutrient, such as calcium or iron, results in the eating of non-food substances that contain these nutrients. Much of this behaviour appears to be based on superstitions, customs and traditions that one often passes from mother to daughter.

Weight Gain During Pregnancy

All pregnancies should be started with BMI of 20-26 because maternal and foetal consequences occur at both extremes. Optional weight gain is about 11 to 13 kg. About 900 to 1800 g is an average gain during the first trimester. Thereafter 450 g/week during the remainder of the pregnancy is usual. Sharp sudden increase in weight after the 20th week of pregnancy, which may indicate excessive, abnormal water retention should be watched. Weight reduction should never be undertaken during pregnancy. Excessive weight gain places an extra strain on the organs and increases the incidence to toxaemia. It is not correct for the mother to think that low gain in weight results in smaller baby which is easy to deliver.

COMPLICATIONS

Anaemia

Too little space between births or too many infections and too little intake of nutrients involved in erythropoisis during pregnancy leads to anaemia.

Physiological changes in the blood occur progressively during normal pregnancy. Haemoglobin mass increases, red blood cell volume increases, plasma volume rises and haemoglobin concentration drops from 13.4 to 11.6 g per 100 ml. Severe anaemia in pregnant women increases maternal morbidity and mortality and involves a higher risk of the foetus. A pregnant woman is labelled anaemic if from the 28th week onwards the haemoglobin is less than 10 g per 100 ml of blood.

A significant fall in birth weight due to increase in prematurity rate and intrauterine growth retardation has been reported to occur when maternal haemoglobin level falls below 8 g.dl. Anaemic pregnant women are prone to urinary infections. The effect of anaemia and urinary tract infection in pregnancy could also be the cause of low birth weight infant.

The predominantly cereal diet in the tropics should be able to provide 40 mg iron per day. Treatment of highly deficient states requires daily therapeutic doses of 120 to 200 mg. This oral therapy may be continued for 3-6 months after anaemia has been corrected in order to replenish the depleted stones. Administration orally of 60 mg elemental iron and 500 μg of folic acid per day in the last trimester of pregnancy prevents anaemia.

The demand for folate is increased because of increased cellular proliferation. The low folate levels are due to deficient intake. Folates are easily destroyed by cooking, hence fresh vegetables should be included in the diet of pregnant woman. Megaloblastic anaemia results in intensified nausea, vomiting and anorexia. A supplement of 5 mg of folic acid ensures an adequate supply for prophylactic purposes.

Anaemia due to B_{12} deficiency in pregnancy is uncommon. A single injection of 40 mcg of B_{12} is enough to produce a maximum response in 10 days in B_{12} deficient mothers.

Pregnancy Induced Hypertension (toxaemia)

Studies conducted at National Institute of Nutrition (1992-93) indicate that severe pregnancy induced hypertension (eclampsia) are associated with higher incidence of vitamin A and protein deficiencies resulting in poor pregnancy outcome.

It is common among women subsisting on inadequate diets with little or no prenatal care. The symptoms of PIH include hypertension, abnormal and excessive oedema, albuminuria, convulsions or coma. Optimal nutrition is a fundamental aspect of therapy. Emphasis is given to adequate dietary protein.

Correction of plasma protein deficits stimulates normal operation of the capillary fluid shift mechanism and circulation of fluid tissue with subsequent correction of the hypovolaemia (abnormal reduction in volume of circulatory plasma). In addition, adequate salt and sources of vitamins and minerals are needed for correction and maintenance of metabolic balance.

In severe pre-eclampisa, oral feeding is suspended in favour of intravenous infusion with 10 per cent dextrose drip during which the patient remains in sedation. Then oral feeding with 10 per cent dextrose, barley and fruit juice is allowed. Bedrest is advocated.

Hypertension

This can cause considerable maternal and foetal consequences. Nutritional therapy will centre on: (1) prevention of weight extremes, underweight or obesity; (2) correction of any dietary deficiencies and maintenance of optimal nutritional stauts during pregnancy; and (3) management of any related preexisting disease such as diabetes mellitus. Sodium intake may be moderate but should not be unduly restricted.

Diabetes Mellitus

During pregnancy glycosuria is not uncommon, because of the increased circulating blood volume and its load of metabolites. Most of these women revert to normal glucose tolerance after delivery.

Prenatal exercise improves fitness, prevents gestational diabetes, facilitates labour and reduces stress.

Keeping in view the above facts the present study was, therefore, assigned to test the tenability of these assumptions through empirical analysis with the following specific objectives :

1. To study the socio-economic status of pregnant women.

2. To assess the clinical and Anthropometric measurement of pregnant women.
3. To assess the dietary pattern of pregnant women using food frequency and 24 hour call method.
4. To identify underutilized foods being consumed by local people of U.P.
5. To assess the micronutrients content, Fe, Cu, Mg and Zinc in identified underutilized food.

Limitation of the Study

Women owing to the physiological needs of pregnancy are particularly vulnerable to nutritional problems. During this period, expectant mothers have to take the nutritious food but on account of ignorance they do not consume as much nutritious diet as is required for pregnant women. There are several factors responsible for this state but the major factors are mal-distribution of essential food commodities, low purchasing power, large families size and limited access to health care families.

CHAPTER

Review of Literature

Review of literature is very important for any type of research work. A brief review available literature is presented in this chapter, which provides a basis for theoretical framework and interpretation of findings.

McPhail and Bothwell (1992), the problem of iron deficiency anaemia is widespread and most prevalent among micronutrient deficiencies. It is affecting an estimated 2000 million people in the world both in developed and developing countries.

WHO (1992) information regarding prevalence of anaemia including folic acid and vitamin B_{12} show that serum folic acid level below 3 μg/ml was highest in Srilanka i.e. 57 per cent followed by India 41.06 per cent, 60-70 per cent of pregnant women has folate level < 125 μg/ml in red blood corpuscles, and is closely involved in the growth and multiplication of cell and also have adverse affect on pregnancy outcome. The adverse affects has been associated with megaloblastic anaemia. The recent demonstration of the causal role of folic acid deficiency in neural type defects. Supplementation of folic acid to pregnant women in developing countries may improve fetal growth and reduces the incidence of low birth weight.

WCD (1995), in India about 58.5 per cent of the total population were malnourished. During course of pregnancy about 28.3 per cent of the women were suffering from malnutrition in which 5.2 per cent were severely malnourished and 22.25 per cent were moderately malnourished.

Goldenberg et al. (1995), zinc deficiency during pregnancy affects not only the mother but it also has immunological consequences for the fetus. Low zinc status is associated with intrauterine growth retardation, neural tube defects.

WHO (1997), criterion was used to define the malnutrition and obesity : (a) malnourished < 18.50 kg/m^2; (b) normal : 19-24.9 kg/m^2; (c) overweight : > 25 kg/m^2; (d) pre-obese : 25-29.9 kg/m^2; (e) class-I obese : 30-34.9 kg/m^2; (f) class-II obese : 35-39.9 kg/m^2; and (g) class-III obese : > 40 kg/m^2. The body mass index is a useful tool in both clinical and public health practice for assessing the nutritional status.

Sachdev, et al. (1997), body mass index is being increasingly used as a measure of nutritional adequacy in adult and is considered as a better indicator of chronic energy deficiency (CED) and the prevalence of chronic energy deficiency was found to be 37-47 per cent in adults.

Umamaheshwari (1997) says maternal anthropometry for prediction of pregnancy outcome was an historic event in the field of maternal health and nutrition. Maternal nutritional factor such as low calorie intake or gestational weight gain, pre-pregnancy weight and height were the most important established determinants of intrauterine growth retardation.

Singh and Singh (1997) stated that profile of rural pregnant women in India showed high prevalence of under nutrition and continuous hard physical work during pregnancy affect their nutritional status.

Umamaheshwari (1997) says maternal nutritional status both prior to and during pregnancy is a critical determinant of pregnancy outcome. Growing fetus derives and store nutrient in liver at the expense of maternal severe under nutrition. If she take restricted amount of food or reduce the amount of protein in the diet there are more chances of fetal growth retardation, thus maternal nutritional status has greater effect on outcome.

Willinghausen and Rink (1997), zinc is an essential element for normal reproduction, growth and development. At molecular level it involved extensively in nucleic acid and protein metabolism. The immune system is influenced by zinc on various levels. Zinc is also important for maturations and functioning of T cells since it is co-factor for thymus hormone thymulin (Hadden, 1992). Zinc deficiency in humans is mainly due to a lack of bio-available zinc in the diet, general malnutrition and a malabsorption (Good, 1981 and Prasad, 1995).

UNICEF (1997), the nutrition and health status of women is important both for the quality of their lives and for the survival and healthy development of their children, yet relatively little attention has been given on this area; further women should not be considered solely with respect to their reproductive roles as mothers, adequate nutrition is a human right for all and the nutritional benefits to women's social and economic capabilities need to be viewed as goals. In recent years renewed emphasis through different governmental programmes (ICDS, RCH etc) have been given to improve the nutritional status of mother, so the present study was planned to assess the maternal nutritional status in rural area. The results of the study are expected to provide baseline for developing suitable interventional strategy for further improvement.

Umamaheswari et al. (1997), copper is widely distributed in biological tissue and largely occur in organic complexes, many of which are metalloproteins and function as an enzyme. Copper containing enzymes are involved in a variety of metabolic reaction such as utilization of O_2 during cell respiration and energy utilization. Copper also involved in synthesis of essential tissue of skeleton and blood vessel and in a range of neuroactive compound concerned in nervous tissue function.

God Frey and Robinsons (1998), during pregnancy a women undergo a remarkable series of physiological adjustment in order to provide fetal growth and development. At same time presence maternal homeostasis concomitantly the fetus exchanges materials with its mother across the placenta via cord and modifies its own development by its maturing regulatory process. At this time minerals play vital role. Element like calcium, iron, magnesium copper and zinc have a key role in protein synthesis and various enzymatic activities, which results in cell growth and multiplication thus leading to a well developed fetus. Thus minerals are important for structural and functional component in the body because of their essential role in cell metabolism.

Vazir (1999), says malnutrition is an ecological problem that does not occur alone, its consorts are poverty, disturbed family structure, ignorance and despair.

Gupta (1999), malnutrition results from imbalance between the needs of the body's and the intake of nutrients. India, gender inequality in nutrition is present from infancy to adulthood. Women never reach their full growth potential due to nutritional deprivation. Malnutrition in women is related to poverty, lack of development, lack of awareness and illiteracy. In the present study, percentage-wise malnourished females are 25.2 per cent as compared to males (20.2%). A wide variety of development actions are needed to improve their food security and nutrition of women.

Kumar et al. (1999) reported that 4-6 per cent of pregnant women complained of nightblindness during pregnancy due to lack of vitamin A in the diet.

West et al. (1999) conducted a study to know that reduction in maternal mortality as a result of supplementation with β carotene or vitamin A in Nepal that striking findings showed that weekly vitamin A or β carotene supplements reduced maternal mortality by 50 per cent in a controlled trial.

Gupta (1999), in developing countries indicates that malnourished individuals, that is, women with a Body Mass Index (BMI) below 18.5 kg/m^2, show a progressive increase in mortality rates as well as increased in 1995, about one million adult deaths resulted from health problems exacerbated by over-nutrition, while half of it were associated with under-nutrition.

Giddens et al. (2000) showed that the percentage of apparently healthy pregnant women with marginal Mg, Ca, folic acid, vitamin C, Zn and Fe intakes was fairly high. Therefore, the potential benefits of a supplementation correcting the sub-deficiencies in apparently healthy pregnant women should not be neglected. The beneficial effects of supplementation in pregnant women suffering from under nutrition and acute micronutrient deficiencies were widely reported in the developing countries.

Ratzan et al. (2000), risks of being underweight (BMI less than 20) may be malnourishment, compromised immune function, respiratory disease, tuberculosis (an infection of the lung), digestive (stomach) disease, cancer, osteoporosis etc. Many factors have been associated with both forms of malnutrition of women in the literature.

King (2000), pregnancy is a critical period in women's life cycle, it is a period of increased metabolic demands with changes in the women's physiology and the requirement of growing fetus.

Gopalan, et al. (2000), in developing countries of the world and more especially in the countries of South Asia including India the major nutritional problem that are now encountered as public health scale are those related to mothers and infants. The latest family health survey data shows a maternal mortality of 540 in India. Thus, more than 100,000 women in India die each year due to pregnancy related causes.

Devi and Sarojini (2000) says diet of pregnant and expectant mother belonging to low income group was deficient in all nutrients and percentage deficit range from 8-63 per cent and reported values showed that lower income group women have poor nutrient intake and poor nutrient intake is reflected by poor nutrition.

Osendarp et al. (2000), trials in developing countries have found that babies whose mother were given zinc supplements in pregnancy have improved influence function and reduction in diarrhoea and respiratory illness in infancy suggesting effects on immune competence that persist beyond birth.

Azais and Posca (2000), maternal malnutrition specially vitamin deficiency is considered to be an important factor contributing to spontaneous abortion by altering germplasm cell morphology. Poor vitamin A status during pregnancy is one of the factor associated with pre maturity and intrauterine growth retardation (Shah *et al.,* 1994). Vitamin A deficiency during gestation can lead to fetal wastage.

School and Johnson et al. (2000), folic acid has long been provided as a supplement in combination with iron during pregnancy on the basis of haematological benefits (Fleming *et al.,* 1986). It's deficiency has been associated with pregnancy complication and congenital malformation.

Gopalan (2000) says vegetables are plant or parts of plant used as food and provide many nutrient beside providing variety to the diet. They are manufacturing organ of a plant where life giving process of photosynthesis occur. They play vital role in human nutrition and are considered to be the cheapest source of minerals and vitamins like β carotene, riboflavin, folic acid, ascorbic acid, iron and calcium (POirie, 1985). Vegetables are excellent component of diet in topical countries (Jijiamma and Prema, 1993). Plant food which could provide several nutrients are in plentiful supply in the country and are of low cost. Traditionally these may be used in various combinations with various physiological status for meeting micronutrient need.

Bharti and Umamaheshwari (2000) stated that there is need to vegetable helps in meeting the demand of food shortage of increasing population and combating micro-nutrient deficiency like anaemia and vitamin A.

Mundra and Mathur (2000) reported that leaf concentrate (commercial product prepared from a variety of green leaves) has tremendous potential for overcoming the problem of anaemia as it rich in iron so its consumption in the daily diet should be encouraged and "Green power must be used in the various supplementary feeding programme run by Government and other Non-Governmental Organizations in our country.

Black, et al. (2001) the latest estimates pertaining to the ICMR multicentric field supplementation trial on 1968 pregnant women lowered these estimates to 62 per cent and 17 per cent. The reason behind this widespread prevalence is due to consumption of diet with differing content and bio-availability of micronutrients and stage of life, economic status, place of residence within a country etc.

Andrew (2001), malnutrition is an ecological problem and affect every stage of life span. Globally round 6,00,000 women die every year from pregnancy related causes and many of them were short, thin and anaemic and have a variety of micro-nutrient deficiency. In developing country like India women are frequently malnourished and often have a poor pregnancy outcome.

Griffiths (2001), BMI is an approximate measure of the best weight for health only. Below 18.5 indicates underweight and possibly malnourished. If BMI is slightly lower, this does not necessarily mean they are underweight. In these instances it is important to consult a dietitian who will provide advice on the best weight to aim for. Women have different nutritional needs in different stages of their life. Much of this work should be done to improve women's nutritional status.

Gueri (2001), the weight for height by week of pregnancy has been devised on theoretical grounds, based on the premises that the average increment of weight during pregnancy is 20 per cent of the pre-pregnant weight and that almost all the increment takes place linearly during the 2nd and 3rd trimesters of pregnancy. The table was tested with retrospective e clinic and hospital data. The results show a good correlation between the weight-for-height at different stages of pregnancy as a percentage of the reference table and the birth weight of the offsprings. This reference table can be a useful tool to assess the nutritional status of pregnant women and, within limits to 'predict' the chances of delivering a low birth weight infant.

Black (2001), vitamins and minerals referred to collectively as micronutrient. Micronutrients have important influence on the health of pregnant women and growing fetus.

Mathuravalli and Co-worker (2001) conducted study to know effect of socio-economic status on nutritional status of pregnant women and pregnancy outcome in selected urban slums of Madurai district reported that as income increases the nutrient intake also increase, and actual daily intake as compared with the ICMR recommended dietary allowances were deficient in various nutrients except thiamin, riboflavin and niacin, iron and calcium intake were also deficient due to less frequent use of green leafy vegetable and only 33 per cent of the estimated population frequently use green leafy vegetable so for increasing nutrient intake people must be aware of locally available vegetable and their consumption in ample amount.

Nuccia, et al. (2001), 13 maternal nutritional status is an important determinant of pregnancy outcomes since pre-pregnancy underweight has been traditionally considered a risk factor for adverse gestation outcomes. Obesity also increases pregnancy complications, such as gestational diabetes, hypertensive disorders, and perinatal morbi-mortality.

Monteiro et al. (2002), body mass index is an accepted measure of chronic energy deficiency malnutrition. Under nutrition remains the nutrition problem of greatest concern in developing countries.

Mortorell et al. (2002), the prevalence of malnutrition (includes both under-nutrition and over-nutrition) among women in Keralaits quite high. Under nutrition remains the nutrition problem of greatest concern which is an important determinant of health and an important outcome of ill health. Differential treatment of girls and boys in terms of feeding practices and access to health care is among the factors responsible for higher female mortality. As a consequence of their lower status overall, women experience discrimination in the allocation of household resources including food and access to health services.

Gautam, et al. (2002), the mean intake of macronutrients and micronutrients, namely, iron, folic acid and vitamin C which play an important role in the pathophysiology of nutritional anaemia during pregnancy was calculated form the foodstuffs, using Nutritive Value of Indian Foods. The preferences and avoidance of various foods by the pregnant women were also elicited. The intakes of calories, protein, iron, folic acid and vitamin C was found to be less than the recommended dietary allowance in 100 per cent, 91.2 per cent, 98.2 per cent, 99.1 per cent and 65.8 per cent of pregnant women respectively. Folic acid intakes were significantly lower in younger, primiparous and poorly educated women from low-income families. Vitamin C intake was lower among non-Hindus only.

Sudesh et al. (2002) intakes of cereal, pulses, roots and tubers, other vegetables and sugar and jaggery by the rural pregnant women were significantly lower than the prescribed Indian recommended dietary intakes. The consumption of milk and milk products and fats and oils was significantly higher than that of RDI whereas, green leafy vegetables and fruits were the most limited food items. As the diets of rural pregnant women were inadequate with respect to some food groups which resulted in lower intake of protein, β-carotene and ascorbic acid. Despite their poor intake their weights and heights were not much below the standards. BMI classification projected that only about one fourth of the respondents were underweight. There is pressing need to educate rural pregnant women regarding their increased nutritional requirements.

Chaudhuri (2002) stated that CINI's current strategy has shown positive trends in improving the health and nutrition status of women, children, and adolescents in the community. Results include reduction of low birth weight babies, increase in proper antenatal care, reduction of severely malnourished children, decrease in maternal and infant mortality and morbidity rates, and improvement in community involvement in all reproductive and child health programmes. CINI is currently monitoring its performance and activities to carryout operations research for providing further evidence for the effectiveness of its interventions.

Hininger, et al. (2002) show that alterations of mineral, trace element and vitamin status are well documented in pregnant women in relation with physiological, metabolic and hormonal changes. The requirements for many micronutrients increase during pregnancy and the risk of maternal deficiencies must be considered since a marginal maternal status can adversely affect the obstetrical outcome.

Andersen, et al. (2002), the women's diet (without supplements) was insufficient in energy and all nutrients except fat, compared with the Indian recommendations. Aggravating low intakes of micronutrients were found which were reflected in low intakes of foods other than rice. Eating customs and economy appeared to influence the women's food choice negatively in relation to recommendations while factors such as education level, family type, pregnancy number and folk dietetics did not seem to have a negative effect. The amounts of foods recommended, especially green leafy vegetables, must be shown to the women. The nutrition advice given by the levels of health providers must be the same and based on cheap, local, commonly consumed foods.

Jaydev (2002), malnutrition remains a silent emergency in India where more than half of all children under the age of four are malnourished. 30 per cent of new born are significantly under weight and 60 per cent women are anaemic (World Bank, 2003). India is a home to about 40 per cent of the world's malnourished children and more than half of her pregnant mothers are anaemic and malnourished.

Gopalan and Patnaik (2002), there are a number of observation pointing to role of essential fatty acid in pregnancy, according to some estimates the average total accretion of essential fatty acid during normal pregnancy of well-nourished women could be amount to 600 g.

Rouse (2003), the oppression of women socially and culturally means they have less access to everything, including food, resources, health care, community support and information. The problems arise from cultural, political and economic realities that must be addressed in tandem. However, one significant step should be taken to educate and to make them aware contribute to struggle against terrible problem of malnutrition. Malnutrition among women has long been recognized as a serious problem in India, but national level data on levels and causes of malnutrition have been scarce.

Lomborg (2004) malnutrition and its associated disease conditions can be caused by eating too little, eating too much, or eating an unbalanced diet that lacks necessary nutrients. Under nutrition, defined as failure to consume adequate energy, protein, and micronutrients to meet basic requirements for body maintenance, growth, and development. Malnutrition is one of the most devastating problems worldwide and is inextricably linked with poverty.

Zulfiqar et al. (2004), while malnutrition in India is prevalent among all segments of the population but poor nutrition among women begins in infancy and continues throughout their lifetimes. Women and girls are typically the last to eat in a family; thus, if there is not enough food they are the one's to suffer most. Children of illiterate mothers are three times as likely to be severely undernourished as children of mothers with at least a high school education.

International Journal of Food Science and Nutrition (2004), average daily food intakes of 90 rural pregnant women of farming and non-farming communities of Northern India were determined. As a result of questionnaires and interviews, food intakes for three consecutive days were collected. Intakes of cereals, pulses, roots and tubers and sugar and jaggery, by both farming and non-farming females were significantly lower than the prescribed Indian recommended dietary intakes (RDI). The consumption of milk and milk products and fats and oils was adequate whereas green leafy vegetables and fruits were the most limited food items. No significant overall differences were observed between females from farming and non-farming backgrounds. Level of education did not show significant influence on intakes of different food items. The consumption of fruits and green leafy vegetables increased with the increase in family monthly income. There is a pressing need to educate rural pregnant women regarding their increased nutritional requirements.

Radhakrishna et al. (2004), traditional foods meant for children, pregnant and lactating mothers are being forgotten and biscuits, bread, noodles, instant infant foods of very high cost are getting more popular. The value of traditional foods including coarse grains, *sattu, khichadi, idli, dalia, mutharies, ladoos* etc. need to be revived. These foods contribute fibre, antioxidant vitamins, Beta carotene, vitamin C and Folic acid, which help in preventing diet related chronic disorders like diabetes, hypertension and cancer etc. Adult malnutrition has received much less attention than that of child.

Sachan et al. (2005), vitamin D deficiency is prevalent in India, a finding that is unexpected in a tropical country with abundant sunshine. Vitamin D deficiency during pregnancy has important implications for the newborn and infant. There are few data from India about the prevalence of hypovitaminosis D in pregnancy and in the newborn. Eighty-four per cent of women (84.3% of the subjects had elevated alkaline phosphatase (17% of urban and 7% of rural subjects). Calcium intake was uniformly low, although higher in urban (842 + 459 mg/d) than in rural (549 + 404 mg/d) subjects (P<0.001). Maternal serum 25 ((OH)D correlated positively with cord blood 25 (OH)D ($r = 0.79$, $P < 0.001$) and negatively with PTH ($r = -0.35$, $P < 0.001$). Conclusion : We observed a high prevalence of physiologically self-concept hypo-vitaminosis D among pregnant women and their newborns, the magnitude of which warrants public health intervention.

Begam et al. (2006), a 100 g supplementary food mix providing 16.7 g protein and 520 K. cal of energy was given daily to a group of mothers in their third trimester, until the time of delivery. Another group of pregnant women acted as control. The results indicated a high maternal weight gain in the supplemented group. Moreover, the birth weight, length, head and chest circumstance of the newborn in the supplemented group was also significantly higher as compared to control group.

Guirindola (2006) says that pregnant and breastfeeding women are also vulnerable or at risk to malnutrition because of increased nutrient needs.

Women's childbearing and nurturing responsibilities sometimes work to their disadvantage when they devote most of their time to family and neglect their own health. This makes them vulnerable to malnutrition.

It is important that pregnant and breastfeeding women get full support from loved one's to relieve them of some discomforts related to pregnancy and breastfeeding.

During pregnancy, there are special nutrient needs to meet the demand of the growing fetus whose nourishment depends entirely on the mother's food. These additional nutrients include energy, protein, folate, iron, calcium and iodine that combine to ensure a healthy baby.

The mother's nutrient reserves are usually depleted when her food intake is inadequate. It is a natural mechanism for the growing fetus to use the mother's nutrient reserves to protect the pregnancy outcome, but to the risk of the mother's health. More often, inadequate nutrients from the mother's womb results to baby's low birth weight of less than 2.5 kilograms.

Uttam and Aremu (2007) says that malnutrition is a serious public health problem, particularly in developing countries, link to a substantial increase. Among pregnant women, energy and protein intake is only 78.4 per cent and 84.7 per cent adequate, respectively. For breastfeeding women, energy and protein intake is only 75.0 per cent and 73.9 per cent adequate, respectively. Iron, the nutrient specifically important for maternal blood volume and iron stores of the baby is only 28.8 per cent adequate for pregnant women, and 33.4 per cent adequate for breastfeeding women based on RENI. Mean riboflavin intake does not meet even half of the requirements of pregnant women at 48.1 per cent and of breastfeeding women at 48.5 per cent. Intake of vitamin A, vitamin C, calcium, and thiamin are all less than 80 per cent adequate for both pregnant and lactating women.

UNICEF (2007) fresh fruit and veggies are my choice for a healthy diet, whether you are pregnant or not. Fresh fish and liver are a healthy choice as well. Dark greens, such as spinach, broccoli, asparagus, etc. Stay away from caffeine and sugar as much as possible.

Madeleine (2008), take vitamins taught expectant and new parent education for ten years. She edits Birth and the Family Journal, a medical care providers' and consumers' journal sponsored by the International Childbirth Education Association and the American Society for Psychoprophylaxis in Obstetrics.

Raj (2008), using three case histories, a review of malnutrition caused by calorie and salt restriction and diuretics is made, with special note of the relationship between these factors and toxemia, low birth weight and other obestric complications. A survey of women entering prenatal classes in four geographic areas of the US is reported. We found that between 24 per cent and 79 per cent of women entering prenatal classes are actually dieting to hold the line at their seventh month weight gains. Up to 66 per cent of women were told nothing as to an ideal weight gain by their doctors, and as many as 10 per cent thought the weight gain given was too high. We found that about half of all women surveyed reached whatever they thought was the maximum weight gain by the seventh month of pregnancy, and then dieted to hold the line; up to 7 per cent were trying to lose weight. Sodium restriction is still being prescribed for between 12 and 49 per cent of women in the communities surveyed. Diuretics for late pregnancy edema are seldom prescribed. The physiology of protein-calorie restriction and salt depletion are reviewed, with recommendations for action on the part of childbirth educators.

Irena (2009) women with low increase in body mass during pregnancy delivered newborns with lower anthropometrics parameters. The increase in body weight of one category resulted in statistically significant increase of birth weight by 140.9 g, increase of length by 0.51 cm and in head circumference by 0.27 cm. Increase in body mass during pregnancy is particularly important in the group of women underweight before pregnancy. Change of nutritional habits before and in the course of pregnancy may have beneficial effects for intrauterine fetal development.

Josepth (2009), their nutritional statuses were determined by measuring the Mid Upper Arm Circumference (MUAC) and Tricep Skinfold Thickness (TSKT). About 57.2 and 61.3 per cent of the pregnant women aversed and craved for at least one food, respectively. The association between food aversion and craving was found to be statistically significant ($\chi^2 = 7.36$, $p < 0.05$). While, statistically significant difference in nutritional status was observed among pregnant women that had aversion and those that did not have no significant difference was observed among pregnant women with and without craving for specific food. Culture has influence on the craving and aversion among the pregnant women studied.

Shinta (2009) this study was carried on some of the factors that predispose pregnant women to PEM and hence identify groups at greater risk. A total of 1387 pregnant women (910 in the urban area and 477 in the rural areas) were recruited for the study. Anthropometric indices of weight, height and Body Mass Index (BMI) of the pregnant women were measured and semi-structured questionnaires were used to elicit information on possible predisposing factors such as age, level of education, parity, child spacing etc. Results obtained showed that the mean weight and height of the rural pregnant women, were significantly ($p < 0.0001$) lower than those of the urban pregnant women. The mean BMI of the rural subjects, was also significantly ($p < 0.0027$) lower than that of the urban subjects. Analysis of the effect of age showed that the younger age category (24 years and below) had significantly ($p < 0.0001$) lower mean BMI and higher prevalence of PEM while the effect of level of education showed significantly ($p < 0.006$) lower than mean BMI and higher PEM prevalence among the less educated (no formal and primary education). Those with parity of two, one and primipara showed significantly ($p <0.0175$) lower mean BMI while child spacing did not have any significant effect on both mean BMI and prevalence of PEM. The implications of these findings are discussed and recommendations made on how to tackle the problem.

Valeri (2010) says diabetes is a temporary form of insulin resistance that usually occurs halfway through a pregnancy. It results from excessive hormone production in the body, or the inability of the pancreas make the additional insulin that is needed during pregnancy in women with no previous history of diabetes. Without enough insulin, sugar builds up in the blood to high levels. This is called hyperglycemia. Gestational diabetes affects about four per cent of all pregnant women although it is usually goes away after childbirth. Untreated gestational diabetes can lead to problems for both the mother and the child. Although insulin does not cross through the placenta to the baby sugar and other nutrients do. The treatment of gestational diabetes should start quickly to prevent adverse effects to the mother and the baby. It should aim to keeping blood sugar level equal to those of pregnant women who do not have gestational diabetes. Treatment includes special meal plans and scheduled physical activity as well as daily blood sugar testing, so as to keep it under control.

Haghdoost (2010) says maternal anaemia is an important public health problem, not only in the East Mediterranean Region but also in many other countries worldwide. The results of the present systematic review suggest that prevalence of anemia during pregnancy in Iran is less than what has been reported by WHO; however, there seems to be the need to implement programmes to reach an ideal state of the disease.

Ians (2010) says All pregnant women should be given vitamin D supplements to safeguard there babies' life, as lack of it could be life-threatening for a newborn. She says women who do not have enough vitamin D can experience complications in pregnancy which could be life-threatening for a newborn. It could also lead to the development of diseases such as rickets and other deficiency linked conditions. We believe that the routine provision of a daily supplement throughout pregnancy would significantly decrease the number of mothers who are clearly vitamin D deficient, reducing related serious risks to their babies she added.

Ians (2010) says excessive intake of calcium supplements may have adverse effect on health. Postmenopausal and pregnant women, transplant recipients, patients with bulimia (an eating disorder) and individuals on dialysis face the highest risk of developing the calcium alkali syndrome. This practice increased individual risk of developing dangerously high levels of calcium in the blood, which could cause high blood pressure and even kidney failure. Calcium supplements taken in the recommended amounts are not only safe but are quite beneficial. Taken to excess is the problem.

Ians (2010) says taking vitamin D supplements during pregnancy is not only safe for mother and baby but it can also prevent preterm labour births and infections. In the 1950s and 60s, people were concerned that vitamin D could cause birth defects, according to Carol L. Wagner, lead study author and paediatric researcher at the Medical University of South Carolina. It is now known that vitamin D is important for maternal and infant health, including bone health and immune function. Recent studies have shown that vitamin D deficiency during pregnancy is a serious public health issue. She also looked at the effects of vitamin D supplementation on complications during pregnancy including preeclampsia, gestational diabetes, infections, and preterm labour and birth. Women should take up to 10 times the current recommended dose of vitamin D during pregnancy, experts have said after it was found to cut premature birth by half.

Ani (2010) says taking a multivitamin pills during pregnancy can dramatically cut the chances of having an underweight baby. Human nutrition, found cases of small-for-gestational age (SGA) births were less than half as common in mothers who had taken 'multiple micronutrient supplements' during pregnancy, when compared with a placebo group. The results of the study showed 'significant levels' of vitamin and mineral deficiency during early pregnancy, with 72 per cent of the group being deficient in vitamin D at the beginning of the study. In addition, 13 per cent were anaemic and 12 per cent were lacking in sufficient thiamin which is needed for healthy nerves and muscles.

Mothers who took the supplement were found to have improved levels of iron and vitamin D by the third trimester. In late pregnancy, 55 per cent of women taking the placebo were anaemic, compared with 36 per cent of those taking the supplement. As to birth weight, eight of 88 babies born to mothers using the supplements were underweight. This compares with 13 of the 61 women in the placebo group.

Ani (2010) says vitamin C and E supplements are of no help when taken in early pregnancy to reduce the risk for the hypertensive disorders and their complications that occur during pregnancy. The study concluded only women giving birth for the first time, a group at higher risk for developing hypertensive disorders of pregnancy. In general, the women were healthy and did not have high blood pressure, protein in the urine (an indication of stress on the kidneys), or gestational diabetes (a form of diabetes that emerges in pregnancy). The researchers enrolled over 10,000 women, starting in the ninth to 16th weeks of pregnancy, and followed them to delivery. The women also received daily supplements of vitamins C and E or a placebo.

CHAPTER

Profile of the Study Area

Prior to discuss the findings of the study on "Identification of under utilized food to combat malnutrition among pregnant women", it is essential to sketch briefly the salient features of the study area. The following are the brief features of district Farrukhabad.

Origin of Name of District

The district is named Farrukhabad after its chief town. The story goes that Muhammad Khan Bangash, the Nawab of Farrukhabad, founded the towns of Kaimganj and Mohammadabad. The former being named after his eldest son and the latter after himself. Farrukhsiyar, the emperor, was annoyed at the Nawab's Presumptuousness in naming a town after himself. To appear his wrath, the Nawab anounced his intention of founding another town and naming it after the emperor. About this time his father-in-law Kasim Khan Bangash, while on his way to Mau, was set upon and killed by a party of Bamtela. Marauders at the village of Jamalpur, now know as Kasim Bagh some 5-km to the east of the town. Using this event as a pretext, Muhammad Khan asked for and obtained a grant of fifty-two Bamtola village for the site of a new town which was founded in 1714 and named Farrukhabad after the name of emperor.

LOCATION, BOUNDARIES, AREA AND POPULATION

Location and Boundaries

In shape the district may be roughly likened to a very irregular parallelogram, situated between Lat. 26°43′ N and Long. 79°7′ E and 80°2′ E. It is situated towards the north-west of the Kanpur Division and is bounded by Budaun and Shahjahanpur on the north, part of Shahjahanpur and Hardoi on the east Kannauj on the south-east, Etawah on the south and Mainpuri and Etah on the west. Its maximum length from north to south is about 120-km and the maximum breadth from east to west about 65-km.

Area

According to the central statistical organization, the district occupied 2333.1 sq.km. in 1991. According to the board of revenue, the area for the same year was 2333.1 sq km. owing to the action of the Ganga in shifting its bed from year to year the total area varies slightly but such changes are usually not very extensive. It is only in the northern portion of Kaimganj and the shifting of the river affects the district as a whole.

Population

According to the census of 2001, the population of the district is 1570408 total urban population, females population is 7,20,608 and male population is 8,49,800. The district stands 28th in the state in respect of population.

Subdivisions, Tahsils and Thanas

The district is divided into three subdivisions, Kaimganj, Farrukhabad and Amratpur.

Tahsil Kaimganj the northern most tahsil of the district is bounded by district Budaun and Shahjahanpur on the north and Tahsil Farrukhabad on the east and south. On the west lies the district of Etah. It has an area of 947.7 sq.km. and a population of 2,98,381 (Females 1,33,644), the rural population being 2,83,227 (Females 1,26,537) and the urban population 15,154 (Females 7,107). There are in the tahsil 398 inhabited and 45 uninhabited villages and one town that of Kaimganj.

Tahsil Farrukhabad is bounded on the north by Kaimganj and tahsil Amratpur, on the east by district Shahjahanpur and Hardoi. On the south district Kannauj. The western boundary is formed partly by district Etah and partly by district Mainpuri. Its area is 1,247.1 sq.km. and the population of 5,31,316 (Females 2,37,612), the rural population being 4,20,481 (Females 1,87,204) and the urban population 1,10,835 (Females 50,408). There are 515 inhabited and 63 uninhabited villages and the township of Farrukhabad-cum-Fatehgarh in the tahsil.

Tahsil Amratpur is bounded on the north by district Shahjahanpur. On the east district Hardoi. The Ramganga forming the eastern boundary for a considerable distance. On the south tahsil Farrukhabad. The western boundary is formed partly by tahsil Farrukhabad and partly by tahsil Kaimganj. The total population of Amratpur 150988 (Females 67698).

Topography

The district is a level plain varied only by a few gentle undulations and slppes. Sometimes gradual and sometimes abrupt, which lead down to the river valleys. The highest recorded elevation is 167 m. above sea level at Muhammadabad and the lowest 145.69 m. at Mau-Rasulpur in the trans Ganga flats of tehsil Farrukhabad. The only marked variation of level is between the two divisions. The upland or bangar, which is a continuation of the doab and the lowlands or tarais, cut away from the upland by the erosive action of the rivers.

Uplands

Lowlands

River System and Water Resources

The principal rivers and streams of the district are the Ganga, Ramganga, Kali Nadi, Isan, Burhiganga or old Ganga, Bagar, Pandu and Rind or Arind.

The first four alone are perennial, the rest being mere channels for the escape of surplus drainage, which cease to flow soon after the close of monsoon.

Ganga	Ramganga
Kali Nadi	Isan
Burhiganga	Bagar
Arind (Rind)	Pandu
Laikes	

Climate

The climate of the district is characterised by a hot dry summer and a pleasant cold season. The year may be divided into four seasons. The cold season, from about the middle of November to February, is followed by the summer season from March to about the middle of June. The period from mid-June to about the end of September is the south west monsoon season. October and the first half of November constitutes the post monsoon season.

Rainfall

Records of rainfall in the district are available for fairly long periods for eight stations—Farrukhabad, Kaimganj, Chhibramau, Kannauj, Digri, Fatehgarh, Aligarh and Tirwa. The details of rainfall at these stations and for the district as a whole are given in the statement II appended at the end of the chapter. The average annual or normal rainfall in the district is 789.8 mm. The rainfall increases in general from west to east, varying from 753.4 mm at Aligarh to 832.4 mm at Fatehgarh. About 88 per cent of the annual normal rainfall is received during the south-west monsoon months (June to

September). July and August are the rainiest months. The variation in the rainfall from year to year is appreciable. In the fifty-year period from 1901-1950, the highest annual rainfall amounting to 180 per cent of the normal, occurred in 1936. The lowest annual rainfall, which was only 31 per cent of the normal occurred in 1918. The annual rainfall in the district was less than 80 per cent of the normal in 11 years, none of them being consecutive considering the rainfall at individual stations, two consecutive years of rainfall less than 80 per cent of the normal, occurred thrice at Digri and twice at Farrukhabad while at Fatehgarh three consecutive years of such low rainfall occurred once. Two consecutive years of rainfall less than 80 per cent of the normal occurred once at the remaining five station. It will be seen from the following statement that the annual rainfall in the district was between 500 mm and 1,000 mm in 36 years out of the 50 years.

Frequency of Rainfall in the District

On an average, there are 39 rainy days (days with rainfall of 2.5 mm or more) in a year in the district. There is not much variation in the number of rainy days in the district.

Range in mm	Number of years	Range in mm	Number of years
201-300	1	901-1,000	8
301-400	1	1,001-1,100	4
401-500	3	1,101-1,200	3
501-600	5	1,200-1,300	0
601-700	9	1,301-1,400	1
701-800	7	1,401-1,500	1
801-900	7		

The heaviest rainfall in 24 hours recorded at any station in the district was 304.8 mm at Kannauj on October 7, 1927.

Temperature

There is no meteorological observatory in the district. The description, which follows, is based on the records of observatories in the neighbouring district where similar climate conditions prevail. The cold seasons starts by about the middle of November when both day and night temperature begin to decrease rapidly. January is the coldest month with the mean daily minimum temperature at about 8°C and the mean maximum at about 23°C. In association with passing western disturbances, cold waves affect the district and the minimum temperature drop to about the freezing point of water. After February temperature rise rapidly. May is generally the hottest month with the mean daily maximum temperature at about 41°C and the mean daily minimum temperature at about 23°C. In association with passing western disturbances, cold waves affect the district and the minimum temperature drop to about the freezing point of water. After February temperature rise rapidly. May is generally the hottest month with the mean daily maximum temperature at about 41°C and the mean daily minimum at 26°C. Day temperatures sometimes go up to about 48°C on individual days. Afternoon thunder showers which occur on some days bring welcome relief though only temporarily. With the onset of the mansoon by about Mid-June, day temperatures drop appreciably. But the drop in the night temperatures is insignificant and nights continue to be as warm as those of the summer season. After October both day and night temperatures decrease rapidly.

Humidity

In the south west monsoon season the humidity is high. After the withdrawal of the mansoon the humidity decreases steadily. By summer the relative humidities in the afternoons become less than 30 per cent.

Cloudiness

Skies are generally heavily clouded or overcast during the south-west mansoon season. During the rest of the year skies are lightly clouded or clear during the cold season for short spells of the day or two, cloudy skies prevail in association with passing western disturbances.

Winds

Winds are generally light. The predominant direction of the winds is between south-west and north-west throughout the year but in the May and the south west monsoon season winds from directions between north-east and south-east blow on many days.

Selection of Blocks and Localities

District Farrukhabad comprises of seven blocks, out of which two blocks namely, Mohamdabad and Barpur were randomly selected for the purpose of drawing samples. These two blocks provided sufficient number of villages from where indicated size of sample could be drawn. District Farrukhabad comprises of different localities. Out of which 10 localities were randomly selected in this study area.

CHAPTER

Research Methodology

This chapter deals with the research procedures applied in conducting the present study. For convenience, the research methodology has been discussed under the following three sub-heads :

A. Research design

B. Variables and their operationalization

C. Data gathering procedure and statistical techniques used

A. Research Design

It comprises of the following sub-parts

(*i*) Locale of the study

(*ii*) District under study

(*iii*) Selection of blocks

(*iv*) Sample of respondents

(*v*) Pilot study

(*vi*) Pre-testing of instruments

(*vii*) Tools and data collection

(*viii*) Statistical analysis of data

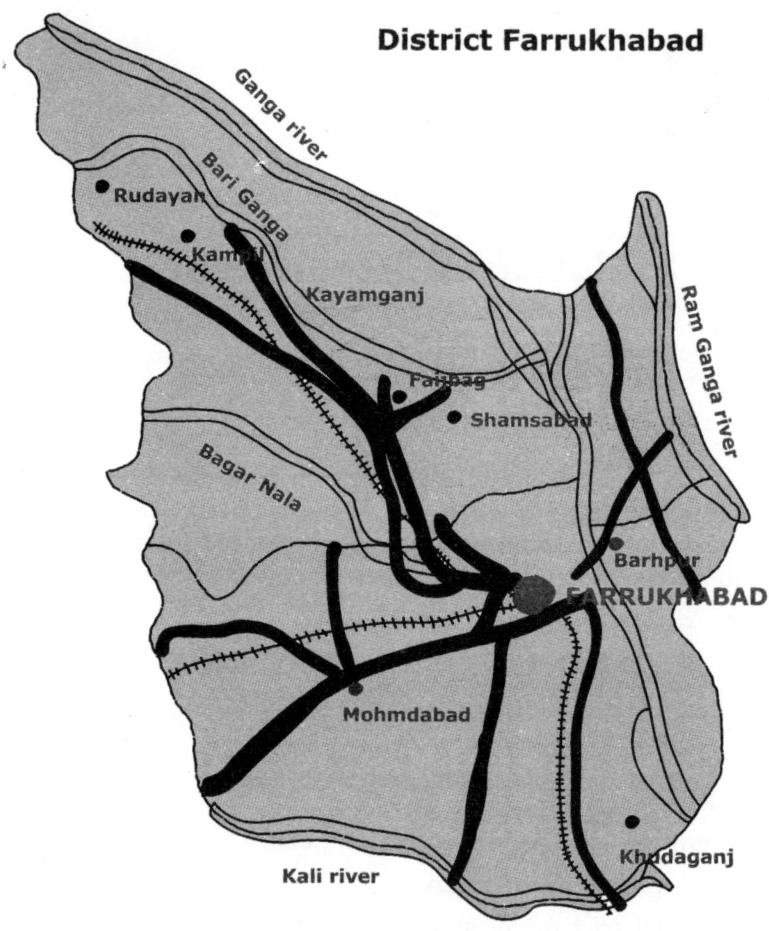
District Farrukhabad
Ganga river
Bari Ganga
Rudayan
Kayamganj
Ram Ganga river
Bagar Nala
Mohmdabad
Kali river

The study was conducted in three parts :

1. Survey method
2. Experimental study
3. Laboratory experiment

(i) Locale of the study : Uttar Pradesh was chosen as locale of the study. This was done with the intension that U.P. is a major state of the country and pregnant women have an important role to play in the development of the state as well as country.

(ii) District under study : District Farrukhabad was purposively selected for this study as the researcher hailed from this place. This helped the investigator to collect the necessary information accurately and timely. The researcher, being from the same place could easily have dialogues and discussions with both during pilot study and final data collection.

(iii) Selection of blocks : District Farrukhabad comprises of seven blocks, out of which two blocks namely, Mohamdabad and Barpur were randomly selected for the purpose of drawing samples. These two blocks provided sufficient number of villages from where indicated size of sample could be drawn.

(iv) Villages identified for the study : In order to identify sufficient number of villages for drawing an appropriate size of samples, a list of total villages falling in the blocks was prepared separately for each of the two blocks. From each of the two blocks five village situated at a distance were selected with the help of systematic random sampling method. Thus, a total of ten villages (five from each block) were selected. For the purpose of drawing the sample of respondents. Block-wise list of all the ten selected villages is given below :

Block Mohamdabad	Block Barpur
1. Gaisinghpur	1. Arrapahadpur
2. Maudha	2. Amethi Jadeed
3. Kanhepur	3. Masaini
4. Neev Karori	4. Jasmi
5. Ukhara	5. Bijadharpur

(v) Selection of locality : District Farrukhabad comprises of different locality. Out of which 10 localities were randomly selected for this study area.

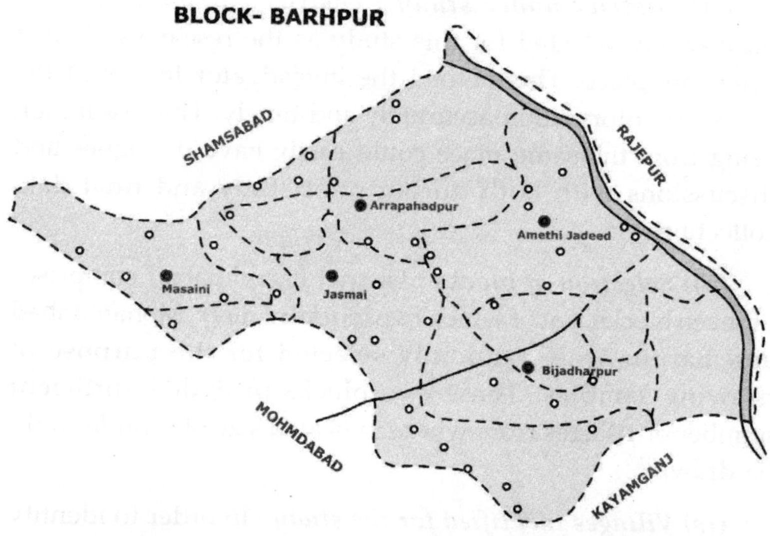

(vi) Selection of Pregnant women : Pregnant women wards selected block in wards 110 pregnant women from rural areas and 110 pregnant women from urban areas were selected. Thus 220 pregnant women were selected randomly in selected area.

2. Experimental study : The different methods were used in study area

(*i*) Clinical examination

(*ii*) Anthropometrical measurement

(*iii*) Dietary survey

3. Laboratory methods

(*i*) Moisture content

(*ii*) Micronutrient content

(vii) Pilot study : Prior to finally deciding the title of the project, a pilot survey of the area was conducted. This gave an idea about the place of the study and nature of the samples that could be drawn and type of aspects and problems which could be explored out.

(viii) Pre-testing of instruments : Before collecting the necessary data from the finally selected sample of 220 pregnant women, 20 people was identified other than those included in the final sample of respondents. These 220 pregnant women were interviewed with the help of schedules and questionnaires developed for collecting the data. This helped the investigator in making necessary changes in the instruments to be finally used their wording and composition.

BLOCK-MOHMDABAD

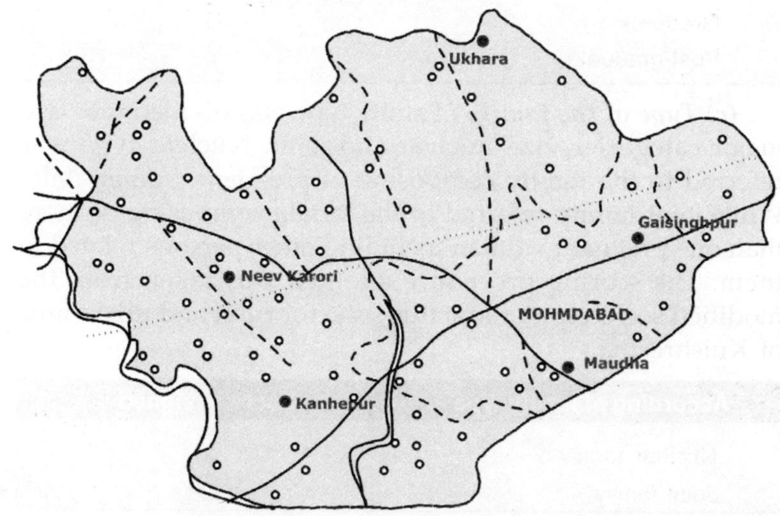

B. VARIABLES AND THEIR MEASUREMENTS

(i) Independent variables *(a) Age* : The chronological age of pregnant women at the time of investigation was taken. All pregnant women were listed according to following age groups and given the scores as follows :

Age-group (years)	Score assigned
18 – 26	1
26 – 34	2
34 – 42	3

(b) Educational qualification : Education was operationalized as the number of years of formal education obtained by the respondents. Scores assigned to different categories on the basis o modified Kulshrestha's socio-economic status (SES) scale for rural was as follows :

Educational qualification	Score assigned
Up to Primary	1
Secondary	2
High School	3
Intermediate	4
Graduate	5
Post-graduate	6

(c) Type of the family : Family type was divided into two major categories viz., nuclear and joint. Nuclear type was referred to the family composing of pregnant women only. While joint family referred to the family composing of more than one pregnant woman including other persons related to them. The scoring procedure adopted was taken from the modified socio-economic status scale for rural and urban area of Kulshrestha.

According of family type	Score assigned
Nuclear family	1
Joint family	2

(d) ***Caste :*** Cast of the respondents in the study was measured on the basis of response of individual pregnant women to which they belong, i.e. in terms of upper caste, lower caste and middle caste. The scores were assigned as :

Caste	Score assigned
Upper caste	1
Middle caste	2
Lower caste	3

(e) ***Total income of the pregnant women :*** The amount of money earned by the pregnant women in a month was measured by recording total income of the pregnant women from all sources. The recorded total income per month was divided into four categories on the basis of modified Kulshrestha's socio-economic scale for rural and urban area (1972) as given below :

Income group	Score assigned
Up to ₹ 5,000	1
₹ 5,000 – ₹ 10,000	2
₹ 10,000 – ₹ 15,000	3
₹ 15,000 – ₹ 20,000	4

(f) ***Family occupation :*** This was measured on the basis of the scores allotted to different family occupation in the socio-economic status scale developed by Trivedi (1963).

Occupation	Score assigned
Landless labourer	1
Caste occupation	2
Farming	3
Business	4
Service	5
Housewife	6

(g) Type of house : The house of respondents were categorized and scores were assigned as under :

Type of house	Score assigned
Kachcha	1
Pucca	2
Mixed	3

(i) Participation : It refers to the degree of involvement of a respondent in formal organizations, either as a member or office bearer. This available information was quantified as specified below :

Participation	Score assigned
Member of one organization	1
More than one organization	2
No membership	3

(j) Material possession : This was measured on the basis of the scores allotted to different material possessions

Material possession	Score assigned
Chair and tables	1
Sofa set	2
Steel almirrah	3
Transistor	4
Electric fan	5
Tape recorder	6
Television	7
Refrigerator	8
Sewing machine	9
Electric Iron	10
Cooking gas	11
Two wheeler	12
Four wheeler	13

(*ii*) Dependent variables

(a) Anthropometric measurement : Anthropometric measurement is concerned with the measurement of variation of physical dimension and the gross composition of human body at different age levels and degree of nutrition. All the subjects were measured for weight height and BMI was then calculated.

(a.1) Height : Height was measured with the help of measuring rod having least count of 0.1 cm. The rod was made to stand straight on a leveled ground. The subject was asked to remove foot wear and head wear and to stand erect, near the rod with heals buttocks, shoulders blades and head in a vertical plane touching anthropometric rod. The pin was kept parallel to ground. The height was recorded in centimeter.

(a.2) Weight : A weighing machine was used to weight the subject in kg with least count of 0.5 kg. Weighing balance was placed on levelled ground and adjusted to zero before measurement. The subject was made to stand erect without touching anything on the weighing balance with minimum clothing and weight was recorded in kilogram.

(a.3) BMI : The continuous BMI variable was categorized into low, middle and high categories, as under weight and overweight status offer risk of different public health problems. The BMI was calculated as :

$$\text{BMI} = \frac{\text{Weight (kg)}}{\text{Height (m)}^2}$$

(b) Clinical survey : All the subjects were visually examined for the various disorder in the clinical examination. The method is based on examination for changes believed to be related to inadequate nutrition that can be seen in superficial epithetical tissues especially skin, eyes, hair, clinical examination consist of routine medical history and physical examination. In order to find nutritional adequacy clinical examination was done. Eyes are examined for cataract, myopia, hypermetropea. Hair was examined for normal, hair loss and loss of colour (whiteness). Teeth were examined for normal, caries or tooth loss. Skin was examined for normal, dry loss of luster and wrinkles.

Dietary Pattern

The strong symbolic and cultural influence and emotional reasons for food choices are broad concepts create a particular food habits of an individual or a community. The diets they consumed in a day is reflected in the food choices which is known as dietary pattern.

Nutrient Intake

The proper design for an adequate diet is a variety and amount of different food, sufficient to provide each day the requirement of nutrient. Nutrient intake may be considered under two general headings.

(*i*) the nutritionally adequate or balanced diet which maintains and promotes health and vigour.

(*ii*) special diet prescribed for treatment or prevention of disease state.

Micronutrients

The organic substances presents in small amount in several food stuffs. They have important functions in many of the vital processes of life the refer, essential for health and well being and needed only in small amounts, such organic substances are known as 'micronutrients' such as vitamins, minerals and fibers.

Dietary Survey

A structured interview schedule was developed and pre-tested before use. Data were collected by paying personal visits to the respondents. Information regarding food consumption habit, dietary intake, nutritional intake etc were obtained. For this purpose 24 hours recall method was used in the sense that respondents were advised to provide information on the consumption of various food items of the pregnant women of the day prior to the day of survey. Dietary recall data was not collected after the day of any occasion or fasting. Showing them standard cups, catories, spoons, glass made the standardization and then they were asked that how many cups or catories of the food they have consumed. In this context the data on the amount of various food items were obtained with were later on converted into the form of raw material. It is to be mention here that it is quite difficult to measure the consumption of various food items very accurately because the respondent themselves were not having any accurate records and the information provided by them may be considered only as approximate one.

To calculate the nutrients like energy, protein, and fat, are used comprehensive Food Exchange List, the amount of food in household measures was converted into metric weight and the nutrient intake was calculated according to the Recommended Dietary Allowances (ICMR). Individual food intake of raw food stuffs was calculated by following formula :

$$\text{Individual intake of raw food stuff used in food preparation} = \frac{\text{Total raw quantiy of food stuff used for preparation} \times \text{Individual intake of cooked amount of that prepration}}{\text{Total cooked amount of food preparation}}$$

Food Habits

A pattern of food eaten called food habit. A number of factor influences the food habits these include, educational and economic level of community, availability and cost of foods and social and cultural practices.

Nutrition : The study of foods, diets and food related behaviours and how nutrients are used in the body. People also use the term to describe the food intake of a person.

Balanced diet : A diet that provides an adequate amount and variety of foods to cover a person's energy and nutrient need.

Iron deficiency anaemia : A condition in a person who has a low haemoglobin or haemotocrit level. Iron deficiency is the commonest cause. Lack of folate, vitamin B_{12}, iron and protein. Besides this, additional non-nutritional cause like malaria, hookworm infection, other infections (such as HIV/ AIDS), heavy bleeding and sickle cell disease are also cause of anaemia.

A low level of iron in the blood and other tissues that keeps the body from working properly. It occurs when a person has used up the body's iron stories, and absorbs too little iron from food to cover needs.

Nutrient : Part of the food that is absorbed and used by the body for energy, growth and repair, and protection from disease.

LABORATORY EXPERIMENT

Moisture Content

The moisture content of green leafy vegetable was estimated by using hot air oven method given by (AOAC, 1980).

Principle : Sample is heated at specific temperature for specific period of time and loss of weight is recorded as the moisture content of the sample.

Procedure

(*i*) A thin layer of finally divided asbestos was spread in flat bottom metallic dish and dry at 110°C for 1 hour.

(*ii*) 100 g of weighed fresh leaves sample was sprayed uniformly over the layer.

(*iii*) Maintaining the temperature of oven at 60-65°C for 16-18 hr.

(*iv*) After drying, sample was cooled in desicator and reweighed.

(*v*) The sample was grounded into powder for analysis purpose.

Micronutrient Content

Micronutrient content of sample was determined by Atomic Absorption Spectrophotometer (AAS) method given by Lindsay and Norwell (1978).

Principle

All atoms can absorb light at certain discrete wave length corresponding to the energy requirement of the particular atom, when at ground state the atom absorb than it is transformed into excited state. This energy is measured in relation to the ground state and a particular excited state. Say for example in case of Na may be 2.2 ev (electron volt) above the ground state.

Reagents

(i) Digestion mixture : A triple acid mixture comprising concentrated nitric acid (HNO_3), sulphuric acid (H_2SO_4) and per chloric acid prepared by taking them in the ratio of 9:1:3.

(ii) Stock standard solution : The standard solution of different micronutrient cation should be prepared preferably by using their foil or wire AR grade. Dissolve 1g foil in dilute HCl (1+1) and make the volume to 1 litre with deionized water to 1000 µg/ml (i.e. µg/1 or ppm).

Alternatively stock standard solution can be prepared from analytical grade as described above, the quantity of the salt given in table should be dissolved in a small amount of water followed by shaking. After adding about 5 ml of concentrated sulphuric acid the contents are then diluted to one litre with deionized water.

Table 4.1. Method to prepare stock standard solution of Zn, Cu, Fe and Mn

Element	Concentration of stock	Salt to be used	Quantity to be dissolved in one litre of solution (g)
Zn	1000	Zinc sulphate $ZnSO_4.5H_2O$	4.398
Cu	1000	Cupric sulphate $CuSO_4.5H_2O$	3.928
Fe	1000	Ferrus sulphate $FeSO_4.7H_2O$	4.960
		Ferrus ammonium sulphate	7.028
Mn	1000	Manganese sulphate $MnSO_4.H_2O$	3.076

Working Standard Solution

A working standard solution of 50 µg/ml was prepared for each element of taking 5 ml of stock solution in a 100 ml volumetric flask and making the volume with deionized water. Further series of standard solution should be made in DTPA extracting solution by taking a known volume of the working standard solution in 50 ml with 0.005 MDTPA solution.

The concentration ranges usually required for different elements are :

(*i*) 0, 0.2, 0.4, 0.8 and 1.2 µg/ml for Zn.

(*ii*) 0, 0.2, 0.4, 0.8 and 1.0 µg/ml for Cu.

(*iii*) 0, 2, 4, 6, 8 and 10 µg/ml for Fe.

(*iv*) 0, 1, 2, 3 and 4 µg/ml for Mn.

Procedure

1. *Digestion of plant sample :* For the analysis of micronutrient cation in the plant tissue wet ashing is generally

preferred to and more convenient than dry ashing. The following step must be followed for digestion of samples.

(*a*) Weigh a suitable quantity of the well-processed plant sample and transfer it to in 100 ml conical flask generally 0.5 g for leafy tissue.

(*b*) Add 10-15 ml tri acid mixture and mix it with content and leave it for over night.

(*c*) Place the flask in a hot plate which has been set at the lowest temperature.

(*d*) As soon as the reaction starts, brown fumes of HNO_3 appear. Continue the digestion at low heat until the white fumes start appearing, raise the temperature of the hotplate and digest the content for a few minutes and than digest for 1-2 minutes at full heat of the hot plate.

(*e*) Continue heating the content of the flask, until the refluxing of the H_2SO_4 starts along the neck of the flask. When digestion is complete the content of flask become white as colourless.

(*f*) After completion of the digestion cool the content of the flask, dilute with dionized water and make the final volume of 50 ml.

(*g*) Transfer the content of flask to polythene bottle for analysis purpose.

2. ***Analysis of digest :*** Micronutrient cations concentration in the plant digest can be determined by the use of atomic absorption spectrophotometer (AAS).

Calculation

Micronutrient are calibrated directly to display concentration of the given micronutrient reading had to be multiple with the dilution factor only.

(iii) Data collection procedure and statistical techniques used

(1) Construction of Interview Schedule : The schedule for the present investigation was thus developed in accordance with the methodological procedures described above, keeping in view the objectives of the investigation.

(2) Data collection : The necessary evidences were collected in line with the objectives of the study. All the 220 pregnant women respondents were inclusively approaches by the researcher. By personal contact, all the respondents were interviewed with the help of the structured schedule developed for the study.

(3) Period of investigation : The data collection was initiated from November 2007 to December 2008.

Statistical Analysis

Statistical analyses are procedures used in finding out the numerical value of the whole study. The statistical techniques for data analysis used in the study are as follows:

1. Percentage
2. 't' test
3. Chi-square test
4. Correlation coefficient
5. Arithmetic mean
6. Standard deviation

1. Percentage : Single comparisons were made on the basis of the percentage, for drawing percentages, the frequency of a particular cell was multiplied by 100 and divided by total number of respondents in that particular category to which they belonged.

$$\text{Percentage} = \frac{\text{The sum of all the responses}}{\text{Total number of all the responses}} \times 100$$

2. t' test : It was applied to test the difference between two sample means and when the observations in two set are independent. Following formula is used :

$$r = \frac{\bar{X} - \bar{Y}}{S\sqrt{\frac{1}{n_1} + \frac{1}{n_2}}}$$

where,

S = combined standard deviation from both sets of data

n_1 = number of observation in first set of data

n_2 = number of observation in second set of data

S = combined standard deviation from both sets of data

$$\left[\frac{\Sigma(X_i - \bar{X})^2 + \Sigma(Y_i - Y)^2}{n_1 + n_2 - 2}\right]$$

3. Chi-square test : In order to test the independence of two attribute, a Chi-square test was applied as :

$$\chi^2 = \sum_{i=1}^{n} \frac{(o_i - e_i)^2}{e_i}$$

Where o_i = Observed frequency of ith cell

e_i = Expected frequency of ith cell

I n × *c* contingency table χ^2 calculated χ^2 value is compared at $(r - 1) \times (c - 1)$ degree of freedom with theoretical value of χ^2 on 5 per cent level of significance.

4. Correlation coefficient : Karl Pearson has given a coefficient of correlation for the measurement of linear relationship, which exists between two variables. If X and Y are two variables and if $E(X, Y) \neq 0$ then correlation coefficient (r) is

$$r = \frac{\text{Cov.}(X, Y)}{\sqrt{\text{Var.}(X).\text{Var.}(Y)}}$$

or

$$= \frac{\Sigma xy}{\sqrt{\Sigma x^2.\Sigma y^2}}$$

where, $$\Sigma xy = \left[\Sigma XY - \frac{\Sigma X \Sigma Y}{n}\right]$$

$$\Sigma x^2 = \left[\Sigma X^2 - \frac{(\Sigma X)^2}{n}\right]$$

$$\Sigma y^2 = \left[\Sigma Y^2 - \frac{(\Sigma X)^2}{n}\right]$$

and n = Sample size

Here, one variable is dependent on other. For testing the significance of correlation coefficient (r), t test is applied. Degree of lack of relationship or coefficient of alienation is measured as—

$$K = \sqrt{1 - r^2}$$

5. *Arithmetic mean* : Arithmetic mean is the average used in the present study symbolically,

(i) For ungrouped data

$$\bar{X} = \frac{\Sigma X_i}{N}$$

(ii) For grouped data

$$\bar{X} = \frac{\Sigma f_i X_i}{\Sigma f_i}$$

where,

X = Arithmetic mean

X_1 = i^{th} variable

f_i = i^{th} frequency

Σf_i = Total frequency

6. *Standard deviation (S.D.)* : It is defined as the square root of the means of the squares of the deviations taken from arithmetic mean :

(i) For ungrouped data – S.D. = $\sqrt{1/n\Sigma(\Sigma X_i - \bar{X})^2}$

(ii) For grouped data – S.D. = $\sqrt{1/n\Sigma f_i - (X_i - \bar{X})^2}$

CHAPTER

Findings and Discussion

The experimental results and its discussion have been presented in this chapter. For the purpose of convenience, the presentation has been sub-divided under the following heads :

The socio-economic status of pregnant women:

I. The clinical and anthropometric measurement of pregnant women.

II. The dietary pattern of pregnant women using food frequency and 24 hour call method.

III. Identify underutilized foods being consumed by local people of U.P.

IV. Assess the micronutrients content, Fe, Cu, Mg and Zinc in identified underutilized food.

(A) SOCIO-ECONOMIC STATUS OF PREGNANT WOMEN

Age

Table 5.1. Distribution of pregnant women according to age group

Age group	Rural	Urban	Total
18 – 26 years	65 (59.1)	50 (45.5)	115 (52.3)
26 – 34 years	32 (29.1)	42 (38.2)	74 (33.6)
34 – 42 years	13 (11.8)	18 (16.3)	31 (14.1)
Total	**110 (100.0)**	**110 (100.0)**	**220 (100.0)**
χ^2		**4.114**	**P > 0.05**

(Figures in parenthesis indicate percentage of respective values)

Table 5.1 shows that distribution of pregnant women according to age-group, 59.1 per cent rural pregnant women were belonged to 18 to 26 years age group while 45.5 per cent urban women have same age group. 29.1 per cent rural women have belonged to 26 to 34 years age group whereas 38.2 per cent urban women have belonged to same age group. The observed value of χ^2 (4.114) was non-significant at 5.0 per cent level of significance.

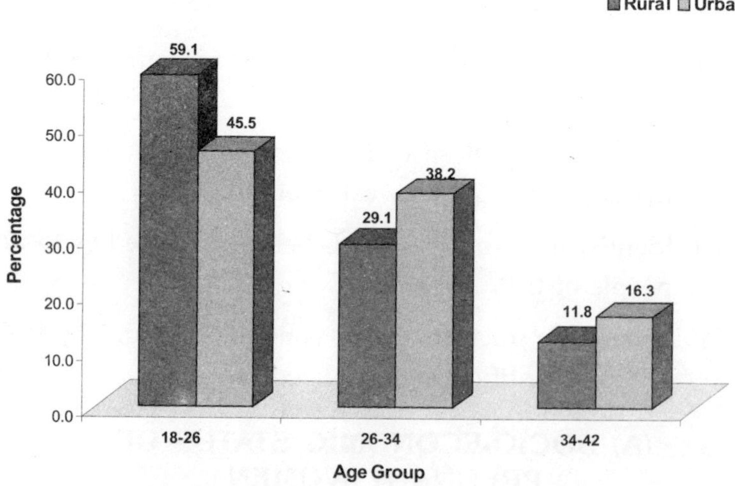

Fig. 5.1 : Distribution of pregnant women according to age group

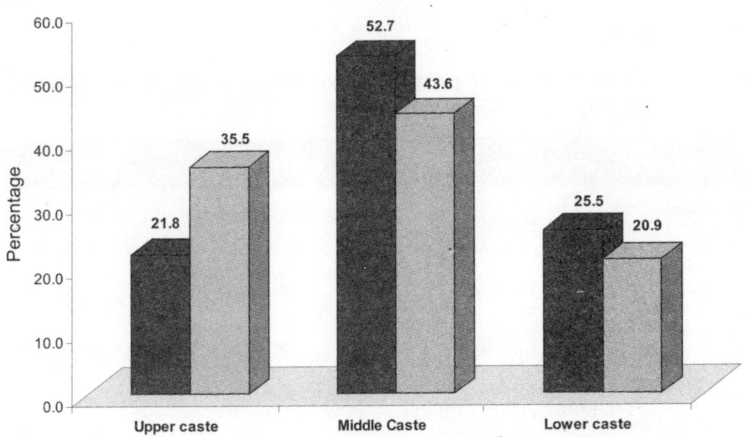

Fig. 5.2 : Distribution of pregnant women according to caste

Caste

Table 5.2. Distribution of pregnant women according to caste

Caste	Rural	Urban	Total
Upper caste	24 (21.8)	39 (35.5)	63 (28.6)
Middle caste	58 (52.7)	48 (43.6)	106 (48.2)
Lower caste	28 (25.5)	23 (20.9)	51 (23.2)
Total	**110 (100.0)**	**110 (100.0)**	**220 (100.0)**
χ^2		**5.005**	**P > 0.05**

(Figures in parenthesis indicate percentage of respective values)

The perusal of Table 5.2 reveals that distribution of pregnant women according to caste, 52.7 per cent rural women and 43.6 per cent urban women were belonged to middle caste while 25.5 per cent rural women and 20.9 per cent urban pregnant women have belonged to lower caste (SC/ST). 21.8 per cent rural women and 35.5 per cent urban women were of upper caste. The observed value of χ^2 (5.005) was non-significant at 5.0 per cent level of significance.

Type of Family

Table 5.3. Distribution of pregnant women according to type of family

Family type	Rural	Urban	Total
Nuclear	52 (47.3)	66 (60.0)	118 (53.6)
Joint	58 (52.7)	44 (40.0)	102 (46.4)
Total	**110 (100.0)**	**110 (100.0)**	**220 (100.0)**
χ^2		**3.583**	**P > 0.05**

(Figures in parenthesis indicate percentage of respective values)

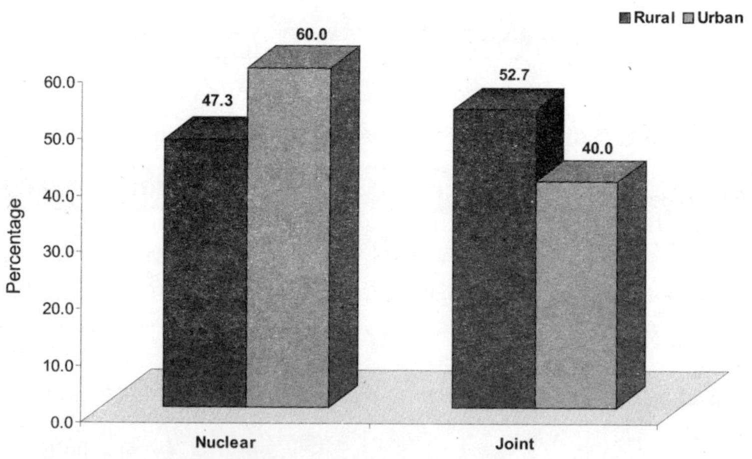

Fig. 5.3 : Distribution of pregnant women according to type of Family

Table 5.3 reveals that distribution of pregnant women according to family type, 47.3 per cent rural pregnant women were belonged to nuclear family and 52.7 per cent rural women have belonged to joint family system. 60.0 per cent urban women have belonged to nuclear family system while 40.0 per cent women in joint family system. The observed value of χ^2 (3.583) was non-significant at 5.0 per cent level of significance.

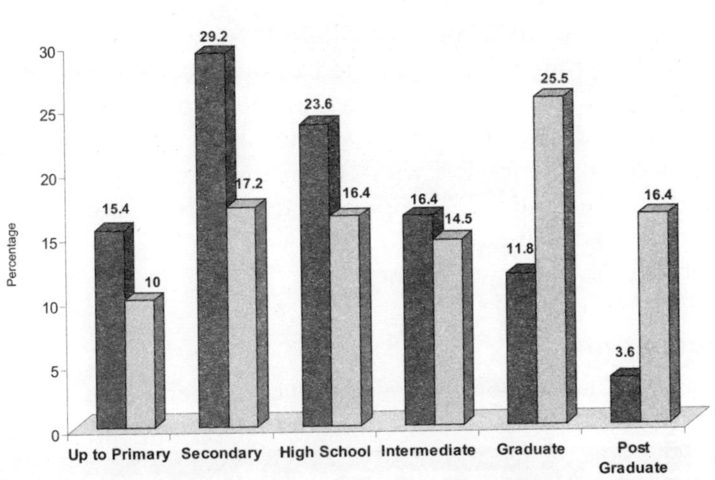

Fig. 5.4 : Distribution of pregnant women according to Education

Education

Table 5.4. Distribution of pregnant women according to education

Education	Rural	Urban	Total
Up to Primary	17 (15.4)	11 (10.0)	28 (12.7)
Secondary	32 (29.2)	19 (17.2)	51 (23.2)
High School	26 (23.6)	18 (16.4)	44 (20.0)
Intermediate	18 (16.4)	16 (14.5)	34 (15.5)
Graduate	13 (11.8)	28 (25.5)	41 (18.6)
Post-graduate	4 (3.6)	18 (16.4)	22 (10.0)
Total	**110 (100.0)**	**110 (100.0)**	**220 (100.0)**
χ^2		**20.568****	**P < 0.01**

(Figures in parenthesis indicate percentage of respective values)

Table 5.4 indicates that distribution of women as per education, 29.2 per cent rural women have passed secondary level education, whereas 25.5 per cent urban women have passed graduate level education. 3.6 per cent rural women have educated up to post-graduate level whereas, 16.4 per cent urban women have educated up to post graduate level. 16.4 per cent rural women were educated up to intermediate whereas, 14.5 per cent urban women have educated up to intermediate. Education wise urban pregnant women were found more educated in comparison to rural pregnant women. The observed value of χ^2 (20.568**) was highly significant at 1 per cent level of significance.

Occupation

Table 5.5. Distribution of pregnant women according to their occupation

Occupation	Rural	Urban	Total
Landless labourer	31 (28.2)	—	31 (14.1)
Caste occupation	24 (21.8)	25 (22.7)	49 (22.3)
Farming	20 (18.3)	—	20 (9.1)
Business	5 (4.5)	4 (3.6)	9 (4.1)
Service	16 (14.5)	38 (34.5)	54 (24.5)
Housewife	14 (12.7)	43 (39.2)	57 (25.9)
Total	**110 (100.0)**	**110 (100.0)**	**220 (100.0)**
χ^2		**50.174****	**P < 0.01**

(Figures in parenthesis indicate percentage of respective values)

Table 5.5 reveals that 28.2 per cent rural women are landless labourers. 21.8 per cent rural women were doing work according to caste occupation like growing vegetables, growing flowers while 22.7 per cent urban women were involved in caste occupation like selling vegetables, selling flowers and washing cloths. 12.7 per cent women (rural) were housewives while 39.2 per cent urban women have housewives. The observed value of χ^2 (50.174**) was significant at 1 per cent level of significance.

Monthly Family Income

Table 5.6. Distribution of pregnant women according to monthly family income

Occupation	Rural	Urban	Total
Up to ₹ 5,000	12 (10.9)	6 (5.5)	18 (8.2)
₹ 5,000 – ₹ 10,000	39 (35.5)	17 (15.5)	56 (25.5)
₹ 10,000 – ₹ 15,000	42 (38.2)	56 (50.9)	98 (44.5)
₹ 15,000 – ₹ 20,000	12 (10.9)	17 (15.5)	29 (13.2)
₹ 20,000 and above	5 (4.5)	14 (12.7)	19 (8.6)
Total	**110 (100.0)**	**110(100.0)**	**220(100.0)**
χ^2		**17.768****	**P < 0.01**

(Figures in parenthesis indicate percentage of respective values)

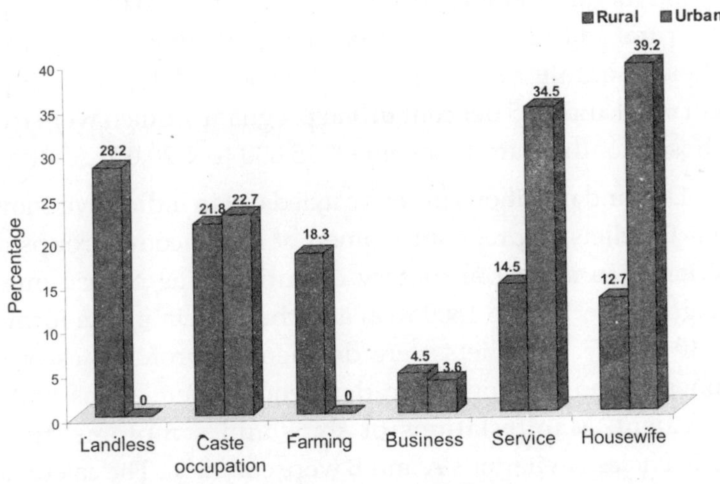

Fig. 5.5 : Distribution of pregnant women according to their occupation

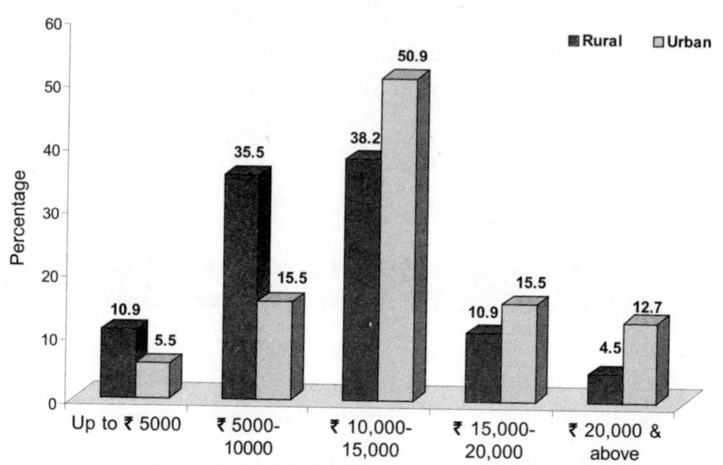

Fig. 5.6 : Distribution of pregnant women according to monthly family income

The perusal of Table 5.6 reveals that distribution of pregnant women according to monthly family income. 38.2 per cent rural and 50.9 per cent urban women were from whose monthly family income ₹ 10,000 to ₹ 15,000. 35.5 per cent rural and 15.5 per cent urban pregnant women were from whose monthly family income ₹ 5,000 to ₹ 10,000 10.9 per cent rural and 15.5 per cent urban pregnant women were from whose monthly family income ₹ 15,000 to ₹ 20,000.

Diet and nutrition surveys carried out in India have shown that the diets of pregnant women of low income groups are deficient in almost al dietary essentials. The calorie intake ranged form 1200 to 1800 Kcal and the protein intake form 30 to 40 g/day. The diets were deficient in proteins, essential minerals and vitamins. Iron deficiency anaemia was widely prevalent. Manifestations of signs and symptoms due to deficiencies of vitamins A and B were common. The calculated value of χ^2 (17.768**) was significant at 1 per cent level. Of significance at 4 d.f.

Type of House

Table 5.7. Distribution of pregnant women according to type of house

Type of house	Rural	Urban	Total
Kachcha	30 (27.2)	08 (7.3)	38 (17.3)
Pucca	40 (36.4)	78 (70.9)	118 (53.6)
Mixed	40 (36.4)	24 (21.8)	64 (29.1)
Total	**110 (100.0)**	**110 (100.0)**	**220 (100.0)**
χ^2		**28.974****	**P > 0.01**

The perusal of Table 5.7 reveals that distribution of pregnant women according to type of house, 36.4 per cent rural pregnant women were lived in pucca and mixed house respectively, whereas 70.9 per cent urban pregnant women have pucca house. In rural area, 27.2 per cent women have kachcha house while 7.3 per cent urban women have kachcha house. The observed value of χ^2 (28.974**) was significant at 1 per cent level of significance at 2 d.f.

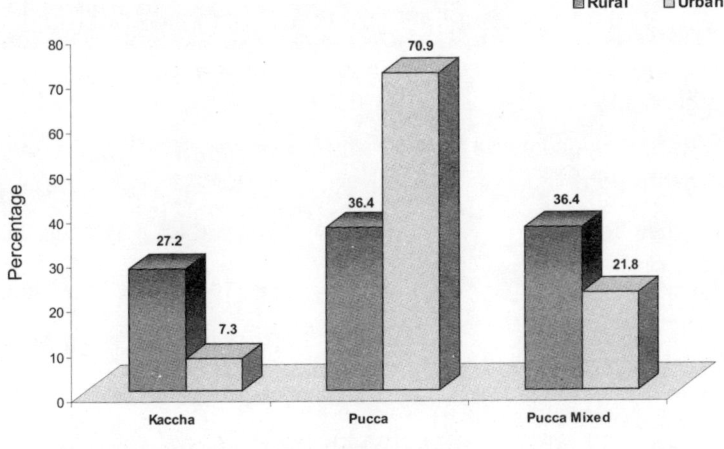

Fig. 5.7 : Distribution of pregnant women according to type of house

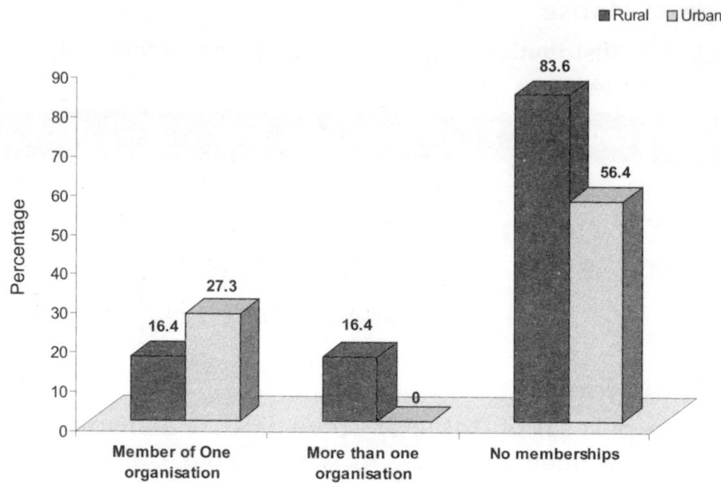

Fig. 5.8 : Distribution of pregnant women according to participation

Participation

Table 5.8. Distribution of pregnant women according to participation

Participation	Rural	Urban	Total
Member of one organization	18 (16.4)	30 (27.3)	48 (21.8)
More than one organization	—	18 (16.4)	18 (8.2)
No membership	92 (83.6)	62 (56.4)	154 (70.0)
Total	**110 (100.0)**	**110 (100.0)**	**220 (100.0)**
χ^2		**19.481****	**P > 0.01**

(Figures in parenthesis indicate percentage of respective values)

Table 5.8 shows that distribution of pregnant women according to participation, 83.6 per cent rural and 56.4 per cent urban pregnant women have no membership in any organization. 27.3 per cent urban and 16.4 per cent rural women were member in one organization. The observed value of χ^2 (19.481**) was highly significant at 1 per cent level of significance at 1 d.f.

Material Possession

Table 5.9. Distribution of respondents according to material possession

Material possession	Rural		Urban	
Chair and tables	77	(70.0)	104	(94.5)
Sofa set	19	(17.3)	46	(41.8)
Steel Almirrah	47	(42.7)	79	(71.8)
Transistor	88	(80.0)	57	(51.8)
Electric fan	89	(80.9)	109	(99.1)
Tape recorder	45	(40.9)	69	(62.7)
Television	80	(72.7)	110	(100.0)
Refrigerator	20	(18.2)	77	(70.0)
Sewing machine	29	(26.4)	52	(47.3)
Electric Iron	18	(16.4)	69	(62.7)
Cooking gas	63	(57.3)	101	(91.8)
Two wheeler	84	(76.4)	100	(90.9)
Four wheeler		—	8	(7.3)

Table 5.9 revealed that distribution of respondents according to material possession, 70.0 per cent rural and 94.5 per cent urban pregnant women have chair and table. Only 17.3 per cent rural and 41.8 per cent urban pregnant women possessed sofa set. Majority of both groups were having electric fan, transistor, television and two wheeler. In urban class most of the respondents have cooking gas, refrigerator, steel almirrah, electric iron and tape recorder.

B. ASSESS THE CLINICAL AND ANTHROPOMETRIC MEASUREMENT OF PREGNANT WOMEN

Table 5.10. Mean height of respondents according to age group

Age group	Rural		Urban	
	N	Height (cm) (mean±S.D.)	N	Height (cm) (mean±S.D.)
18 – 26 years	65	156±5.6	50	158±5.1
26 – 34 years	32	153±3.1	42	152±3.5
34 – 42 years	13	154±2.4	18	153±3.0
Total	**110**	**154±4.7**	**110**	**154±4.9**
r		**0.1273**		**0.2061**

Table 5.10 indicates the mean height of the pregnant women according to their age group. The average mean height 156 cm of the rural pregnant women in age group 18 to 26 years whereas 154 cm mean height of the rural women in age group 34 to 42 years. In urban area a mean height 158 cm of the pregnant women have belonged to age group 18 to 26 years and mean height 152 cm of the women in age group 26 to 34 years. More deviation of the mean height was found in age group 18 to 26 years of both rural and urban areas. There is general agreement that a relationship exists between maternal height and mean birth weight. Adequate nutrition before and during pregnancy has greater potential for a long term health impact than it does at any other time. Maternal health is a complex influenced by various genetic social and economic factors and environmental conditions many of which may affect the foetal growth.

Maternal anthropometry for prediction of pregnancy outcomes was an historic event in the field of maternal health and nutrition. Maternal nutrition factors such as low caloric intake or gestational weight gain, pre-pregnant weight, and height were the most important established determinants of intrauterine growth retardation (IUGR), LBW, perinatal, neonatal and infant mortality and poor infant growth.

Table 5.11. Average weight of the pregnant women according to age group

Age group	Rural		Urban	
	N	Weight (cm) (mean±S.D.)	N	Weight (cm) (mean±S.D.)
18 – 26 years	65	59 ± 5.0	50	63 ± 3.0
26 – 34 years	32	63 ± 4.0	42	65 ± 5.0
34 – 42 years	13	64 ± 4.0	18	68 ± 3.0
Total	**110**	**62 ± 4.0**	**110**	**66 ± 5.0**
r		**3.3136***		**0.4417***

For optimal introutering growth and survival weight gain should be on an average around 9 kg. Both excess or low weight gain are associated with high incidence of prematurity, LBW and perinatal mortality. Undernourished women gain 6.5 to 7 kg during pregnancy. Weight gain below 6 kg is associated with more than 55 per cent of the LBW babies. Adolescent mother require more nutrients than mature women to produce similar size infants, as her own nutrient requirements complete with those of her foetus.

All pregnancies should be started with BMI of 20-26 because maternal and foetal consequences occur at both extremes. Optimal weight gain is about 11 to 13 kg. About 900 to 1800 g is an average gain during the first trimester. Thereafter 450 g/week during the remainder of the pregnancy is usual. Sharp sudden increase in weight after the 20th week of pregnancy, which may indicate excessive, abnormal water retention should be watched. Weight reduction should never be undertaken during pregnancy. Excessive weight gain places an extra strain on the organs and increases the incidence to toxaemia. It is not correct for the mother to think that low gain in weight results in smaller baby which is easy to deliver.

Growth of the foetus of poorly nourished mother is almost similar to the foetus of well nourished mother till the 28th week of gestation. The fat deposits in the foetus occur in the 1st trimester of pregnancy. Fat deposition in the undernourished pregnant women is very minimal in the last trimester, which is responsible for poor fat storage in the foetus. Average birth weight of a healthy term infant of undernourished mother tends to be 500 g or so less than that of a well nourished mother due to lesser deposition of fat.

In adolescent, normal birth weight was associated with increased skin folds and arm circumference, suggesting fat deposition during pregnancy. While those who delivered LBW infants either deposited no fat during pregnancy or showed evidence of mobilizing body fat to meet the needs of the growing foetus.

Maternal triceps skin folds measured shortly after birth were negatively correlated with birth weight, suggesting that the fattest women can gave birth to the smallest infants (Briand, 1985) hypothesised and hypothesized that maternal lean body mass rather than maternal fat stores was associated with fetal growth. Women who begin pregnancy with low pregnancy weights need to gain more weight during pregnancy than women who are of average or over weight. The combination of low pre-pregnancy weight and low weight gain during pregnancy puts women at the greatest risk of delivering of LBW baby (Roso, 1985). Pregnancy weight and pregnancy weight gain are independent and completely additive and subtractive in their effect on birth weight together accounting for a difference of up to 1 kg in birth weight.

Several investigations had been carried out to evaluate simple measurement of fundal height and abdominal girth as a method of assessment of fetal growth. Studies undertaken at NIN had demonstrated that fundal height and abdominal growth show a progressive increase with increasing gestational age, weeks of gestation and there was a varied degree of correlation between fundal height and abdominal girth and birth weight.

Table 5.11 shows that average weight of the pregnant women according to age group, weight of the pregnant women were increased according to age group in both areas rural as well as urban women. 64 kg weight of rural women and 68 kg weight of urban women were belonged to 34 to 42 years of age group. The correlation coefficient 0.3136* positively significant between weight of rural women and her age group. Average weight 66 kg of urban women and correlation coefficient (0.4417*) was significant between weight of urban women and her age group. Women who begins pregnancy with low pregnancy weights need to gain more weight during pregnancy than women who are of average or over weight. Pregnant women undergo a remarkable series of physiological adjustments in order to provide for fetal growth and development and at the same time preserve maternal homeostatly. The above risk factors can be identified in both rural and urban areas in pregnant women at higher risk of delivering low birth weight on the basis of history and simple examination. Two major risk factors were reported in the increasing prevalence in pregnant women who delivered low birth weight infant were, previous bad obstetric history and currently identified obstetric problem. 40 per cent of pregnant women who delivered infants weighing over 2.5 kg at birth had one or more identified risk factors. Prevalence of these risk factors were doubled in a group that delivered infants less than 2.0 kg.

Table 5.12. BMI of pregnant women according to age group

Age group	Rural		Urban	
	N	BMI (mean±S.D.)	N	BMI (mean±S.D.)
18 – 26 years	65	24.2 ± 1.9	50	25.2 ± 1.7
26 – 34 years	32	26.9 ± 1.6	42	28.1 ± 1.8
34 – 42 years	13	27.0 ± 1.6	18	29.0 ± 1.9
Total	**110**	**26.1 ± 1.7**	**110**	**27.8 ± 1.8**
r		**0.2013**		**0.3110***

Table 5.12 shows that average BMI of the pregnant women according to age group, in both areas rural and urban BMI of pregnant women have increased according to age group. 27.0+1.6 BMI of rural women and 29.0+1.9 BMI of urban pregnant women were belonged to 34 to 42 years age group. The correlation coefficient between BMI of urban women and her age group was significant thus according to age group BMI was increased in urban area. Maternal nutritional status, both prior to and during pregnancy is a critical determinant of pregnancy outcomes, a positive and significant relationship between maternal pre-pregnancy weight for height and fetal size has been observed in both well-nourished and poorly nourished populations. The highest risk of delivering a low birth weight infant has been observed among women who begin. Pregnancy with a low weight for height or simply a low pre-pregnancy weight. Thinner women need to gain more weight during pregnancy than average size or heavier women to significantly lower their risk of unfavourable outcomes.

A positive and significant relationship between maternal pre-pregnancy weight or pre-pregnancy weight-for-height (body mass index) and fetal size has been observed in both well-nourished and poorly-nourished populations. The highest risk of delivering a low birth weight infant has been observed among women who begin. Pregnancy with a low weight-for-height or simply a low prepregnancy weight. This risk appears to relate to both IUGR low birth weight and to preterm low birth weight. Prepregnancy obesity is also risk factor for unfavourable pregnancy outcomes such as perinatal mortality, high birth weight (when combined with high pregnancy weight gain) and infant mortality.

Height : There is general agreement that a positive relationship exists between maternal height and mean birth weight, and increased risk of IUGR rather than preterm birth. Marginally nourished mothers, a low maternal head circumference predicted IUGR, but not preterm LBW. Low maternal height and head circumference may reflect maternal stunting secondary to under nutrition during childhood.

Arm circumference : Maternal arm circumference can be used to assess the nutritional status of non-pregnant women as well as prior to or during pregnancy to identify women at risk of LBW and fetal or mortality.

Weight for height and body mass index : Thinner women need to gain more weight during pregnancy than average size or heavier women to significantly lower their risk of unfavourable outcomes such as LBW, small-for-date infants and perinatal mortality. In India, where the average height of pregnant women was 150 cm, found that maternal weight <40 kg was far more predictive of underweight in children than maternal weight for height or a BMI <18 (Anerson, 1989).

Reproductive outcomes in women prenatally exposed to under nutrition : (Dutch famine birth study, affected the Western Netherlands in the winter of 1944-45). The study showed that an acute reduction in intra-uterine nutrition of women have long-term health effect on their off-spring. But these effects critically depend on the timing of exposure in relation to the stage of pregnancy and are mostly dependent on the mother's own birth weight. The study was conducted on women born before, during and after 45 years of the hunger period. There was an increase in the risk of still birth and perinatal death among offspring of women prenatally exposed to famine in the third trimester of pregnancy.

Off-spring birth weight across families : Normally the increase in offspring birth weights was seen with increasing birth order. But within sibship birth weight decreased with increasing birth order among offspring of women exposed to under-nutrition in the 1st trimester of pregnancy.

Clinical examination is based on changes, believed to be related to inadequate nutrition that can be seen or left. Clinical examination was performed to assess the general health status of the subjects and presented in Table 5.13.

Table 5.13. Clinical assessment and symptoms in pregnant women

Clinical assessment	Rural	Urban
Appearance		
Healthy	38 (34.5)	64 (58.2)
Unwell	49 (44.5)	32 (29.1)
Ill	23 (20.9)	14 (12.7)
χ^2	12.385**	P < 0.01
Hair		
Normal	44 (40.0)	54 (49.1)
Lusterless	47 (42.7)	27 (24.5)
Thin and sparse	19 (17.3)	29 (26.4)
χ^2	8.509*	P < 0.01
Lips		
Normal	74 (67.3)	97 (88.2)
Angular stomatitis	28 (25.5)	10 (9.1)
Cheilosis	8 (7.2)	3 (2.7)
χ^2	13.893**	P < 0.01
Tongue		
Normal	55 (50.0)	87 (79.1)
Red and Raw	39 (35.5)	19 (17.3)
Pale	16 (14.5)	4 (3.6)
χ^2	21.308**	P < 0.01
Gum		
Normal	66 (60.0)	80 (72.7)
Bleeding gum	38 (34.5)	13 (11.8)
Swollen	6 (5.5)	17 (15.5)
χ^2	18.858**	P < 0.01

(Contd....)

Clinical assessment	Rural		Urban	
Skin				
Normal	74	(67.3)	99	(90.0)
Dermatitis	17	(15.4)	5	(4.5)
Pallor skin	19	(17.3)	6	(5.5)
χ^2	12.589**		P < 0.01	
Conjuctival symptoms				
Normal	56	(50.9)	99	(90.0)
Bitot spot	21	(19.1)	5	(4.5)
Brown dispigmentation	33	(30.0)	6	(5.5)
χ^2	40.467**		P < 0.01	

(Figures in parenthesis indicate percentage of respective values)

It was found that 44.5 per cent rural pregnant women and 29.1 per cent urban women were reported unwell in terms of nausea and 20.9 per cent rural and 12.7 per cent urban women was found to be ill, at complete bedrest.

Hair examination indicate that 40.0 per cent rural and 49.1 per cent urban women having normal hair, 17.3 per cent rural and 26.4 per cent urban having thin and sparse hair.

Lusterless hair and thin and sparse hair might be due to deficiency of protein in the diet. The value of χ^2 is 8.509 and it is significant at 1 per cent level.

Clinical symptoms observed related to vision include xerosis, bitot spot, brown dipigmentation and pale eyes in cornea and conjunctiva both.

In all subjects cornea was found to be normal and there was no case of dry, hazy and opaque cornea.

Conjuctival signs and symptoms showed that 19.1 per cent rural and 4.5 per cent urban women had bitot spot. 30.0 per cent rural women, 5.5 per cent urban found had brown dipigmentation and rest 50.9 per cent rural and 90.0 urban women were found to be normal.

Kumar (1999) revealed that 4.6 per cent of pregnant women complained of night blindness during pregnancy.

The sign and symptoms of vitamin B_{12} and vitamin C deficiency were also noted through gums, tongue and lips. Lips of pregnant women showed that 67.3 per cent rural women was found to be normal and 25.5 per cent rural women having angular stomatitis and 7.2 per cent had chelosis.

Tongue of pregnant women showed that 50 per cent rural and 79.1 per cent urban women and 35.5 per cent rural women had red and raw tongue and only 14.5 per cent subject was examined having pale tongue showing condition of severe anaemia.

Swami *et al.* (1986) revealed that anaemia was more prevalent amongst illiterate women and those with primary education as compared to women who have higher education.

Signs and symptoms examined related to gums revealed that 60.0 per cent rural and 72.7 per cent urban women, 34.5 per cent rural women were found to be bleeding gum and 5.5 per cent subject was found to have swelling gum. Bleeding gum and swelling gum was due to deficiency of vitamin C in diet.

Mathuravalli (2001) reported that vitamin C deficiency in low socio-economic status was 42.3 per cent due to reflection of inadequate intake of green leafy vegetables and fruits.

Skin changes examination showed that 67.3 per cent rural and 87.3 urban women respondents were normal skin, 15.4 per cent rural women had dermatitis and 17.3 per cent rural women were found to be pallor skin which indicate presence of anaemia and vitamin B deficiency.

There was no case found to had koliongunchia enlargement of thyroid gland, stained teeth etc. in both rural and urban pregnant women.

(C) THE DIETARY PATTERN OF PREGNANT WOMEN USING FOOD FREQUENCY AND 24 HOURS CALL METHOD

General Health and Obstetric Information

Birth Order (Parity number)

Table 5.14. Distribution of respondents on the basis of parity number

Criteria	Rural	Urban	Total
1	7 (6.4)	28 (25.5)	35 (15.9)
2	38 (34.5)	69 (62.7)	107 (48.6)
3	52 (47.3)	10 (9.1)	62 (28.2)
4	8 (7.3)	2 (1.8)	10 (4.5)
5	2 (1.8)	1 (0.9)	3 (1.4)
12	3 (2.7)	—0	3 (1.4)
χ^2		**50.174****	**P < 0.01**

Obstetric and general health information of both rural and urban pregnant women revealed that 15.9 per cent (35) were in parity number 1 and 48.6 per cent (107) were in parity number 2 and 28.2 per cent (62) were in parity number 3 4.5 per cent (10) were found to be in parity number 4 1.4 per cent (3) were in 5th parity and only 1.4 per cent subject was found to have 12 parity number was the exception in all case. Parity was directly or indirectly related to nutrition (Hurlock, 1978) it has significant correlation with education and number of abortion. (*Table 5.14*)

In the present study, (*See Table 5.15*) it was found that 95 (43.2%) pregnant women found to be had no miscarriage case. 66 (30.0%) women had at least one miscarriage and only 1 women was found to had more than 8 times miscarriage. The exact reasons was not known for miscarriage. It was found that parity number and number of miscarriage have significant correlation.

Table 5.15. Distribution of respondents on the basis of miscarriage

Criteria	Rural	Urban	Total
Nil	34 (30.9)	61 (55.5)	95 (43.2)
1	39 (35.5)	27 (24.5)	66 (30.0)
2	29 (26.4)	19 (17.3)	48 (21.8)
3	7 (6.3)	3 (2.7)	10 (4.5)
More than 3	1 (0.9)	—	1 (0.5)
χ^2		14.212**	P < 0.01

(Figures in parenthesis indicate percentage of respective values)

Table 5.16. Distribution of respondents as per birth interval in a year

Birth interval	Rural	Urban	Total
1 year	24 (21.8)	8 (7.3)	32 (14.5)
2 year	43 (39.1)	32 (29.1)	75 (34.1)
3 year	34 (30.9)	23 (20.9)	57 (25.9)
4 year	9 (8.2)	47 (42.7)	56 (25.5)
χ^2		37.522**	P < 0.01

(Figures in parenthesis indicate percentage of respective values)

It was found that birth interval between two children varied from one year to four years. One year birth interval was found in 18 cases, two year birth interval was studied in 10 cases and in 32 cases birth interval was more than two years. (*Table 5.16*).

(B) DIETARY PATTERN OF PREGNANT WOMEN

Food Habits

The perusal of Table 5.17 reveals that distribution of pregnant women according to food habit, 66.4 per cent rural women have vegetarian whereas 47.3 per cent urban pregnant women were taking vegetarian food in her meals. 52.7 per cent urban pregnant women were non-vegetarian whereas 33.6 per cent rural women have non-vegetarian. In comparison to rural women, urban women have taking more non-veg food in meals. The observed value of observed value of χ^2 (8.170**) was highly significant at 1 per cent level of significance.

Table 5.17. Distribution of pregnant women according to food habits

Food habits	Rural	Urban	Total
Vegetarian	73 (66.4)	52 (47.3)	125 (56.8)
Non-vegetarian	37 (33.6)	58 (52.7)	95 (43.2)
Total	110 (100.0)	110 (100.0)	220 (100.0)
χ^2		8.170**	P < 0.01

(Figures in parenthesis indicate percentage of respective values)

Dietary Intake of Pregnant Women

Nutrient requirement in adults are meant mainly as replacement for the losses and there is no need of additional requirements as there will be no growth. On the other hand, the requirements of nutrients in pregnancy and lactation are based upon the factorial approach i.e., in addition to the requirements of the adult female, requirements arising out of the growth of maternal tissues and that of concepts during pregnancy, and secretion of milk during lactation, are considered.

Maternal nutrition plays a role in certain types of fetal malformations or spontaneous abortion. Because these abnormalities occur so early in pregnancy (during organogenesis) modifications must be made before pregnancy begins. In diabetes, incidence of congenital defects can be reduced almost to normal by bringing the blood glucose under good control prior to pregnancy. Administration of folic acid 400-800 mcg per day around and during conception and early gestation can reduce the incidence of neural tube defects. In addition, women with low body weight and poor nutritional status prior to pregnancy have more low birth weight infants, premature spontaneous rupture of membranes, infection and anaemia.

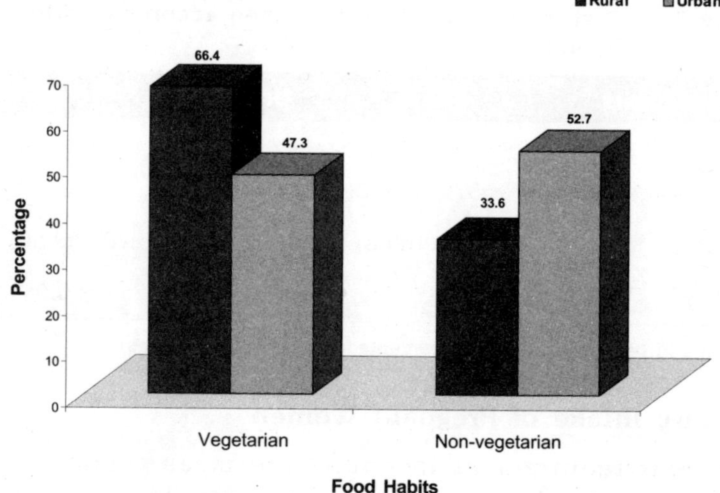

Fig. 5.9 : Distribution of pregnant women according to food habit

On the other end of the spectrum, overweight women are more likely to have fetal death, diabetes, hypertensive disorders and labour abnormalities. Because these maladies are difficult to correct once pregnancy begins, a woman should achieve a body mass within 90-120 per cent of ideal weight prior to conception.

Due to undernourishment of the mother the baby is at an increased risk of being premature with low birth weight and developmental irregularities. Intrauterine nutrition is highly important for the growth of the central nervous system and kidneys of the foetus which mature during the latter part of pregnancy. Therefore, nutrition deficits before birth can never be wholly reversed after birth.

Table 5.18. Daily food intake by rural and urban pregnant women under study period

Food intake	Rural						Urban					
	Vegetarian (g/day) 73	RDA	Deficit/increase %	Non-vegetarian (g/day) 37	RDA	Deficit/increase %	Vegetarian (g/day) 53	RDA	Deficit/Increase %	Non-vegetarian (g/day) 58	RDA	Deficit/Increase %
Cereal	421±22	410	+2.7	410±21	400	+2.5	271±13	280	–3.2	264±15	270	–2.2
Pulses	47±9	60	–21.7	44±13	50	–12.0	74±18	60	+23.3	70±19	50	+40.0
Green leafy vegetables	119±18	100	+19.0	106±19	100	+6.0	78±22	100	–22.0	69±26	100	–31.0
Root and tubers	56±22	100	–44.0	67±18	100	–33.0	62±18	75	–17.3	69±22	75	–8.0
Fruits	62±17	100	–38.0	56±19	100	–44.0	110±20	100	+10.0	102±17	100	+2.0
Milk and its product	635±36	600	+5.8	506±34	400	+26.0	445±40	600	–25.8	339±26	400	–15.2
Fat and oil	53±19	40	+32.5	59±23	45	+31.1	31±7	35	–11.4	35±9	40	–12.5
Sugar and jaggery	49±10	40	+22.5	43±12	40	+7.5	22±8	30	–26.7	19±9	30	–36.7

Table 5.18 reveals that daily food intake by pregnant women under study period, cereals and millets and it's constitute have used in bulk form in Indian diet. Average cereals 42.1 g/day by vegetarian rural women and 271 g/day by urban vegetarian women were taking whereas 410 g/day non-veg rural women and 264 g/day non-veg urban women consumed respectively. Rural women were taking more cereals g/day in comparison to urban women. 106 g/day average GLVs by non-veg rural women and 69 g/day GLVs by non-veg urban women were taking but its deficit by standard value. In Uttar Pradesh mean intake of cereal is significantly less than of 446 g per day as found by ICMR (1989). In rural area, this amount is even less than average intake of urban people. Green leafy vegetable (GLVs) are rich source of iron, calcium, β carotene, vitamin C, riboflavin and folic acid. At least 50 g of green leafy vegetable should be consumed in one's diet. In the present study both areas consumption was less than the comparable amount of 100 g per day.

Roots and tubers are rich in carbohydrates form and an important source of energy to the diet. Mean intake of root and tubers in vegetarian rural women 56+22 g/day and 62+18 g/day urban vegetarian women were consumed. Other vegetable are source of dietary fibre and provide vitamin C and minerals. Other vegetable consumption in rural and urban pregnant women was satisfactory.

Lime, tomato were consumed as fruits while apple, orange and other fruits were not consumed due to its high cost. Banana and guava are often consumed because it was easily available in their orchard. Consumption of fruits per day in vegetarian rural women was 62+17 g/day and 110+20 g/day vegetarian urban women respectively. The intake of milk and milk product was adequate in urban area pregnant women higher than rural area pregnant women. Non vegetarian rural pregnant women were consumed average fats and oil 59+23 g per day whereas in urban area they have taken 35+9 g per day. Consumption of sugar and jaggery more in rural area comparatively urban area. 49+10 g per day sugar and jaggery vegetarian rural pregnant women were consumed whereas 22+8 g/day in urban area. Mean intake of cereals, pulses, GLVs, fruits, milk product and fats and oil significantly different in both rural and urban areas. In urban area cereal, GLVs, milk and its product, fat and oil and sugar and jaggery have consumed more with compared with RDA whereas in urban area pulses and fruits have taken more with compared RDA.

The major cereals and millets consumed in India are rice, wheat (cereals), Jowar, bajra, ragi (millets). In recent years the production and consumption of maize has also increased. These grains are the main source of energy in Indian diets contributing as they do 70-80 per cent of daily energy intake of majority of Indians. Since cereals/millets are the cheapest, widely available source of energy, they contribution to energy intake is the highest among the poor income families and it decreases with increasing income. Even with the highest income groups, cereals account for at least 50-60 per cent of the energy intake. In view of the large intake, cereals are also an important source of several other nutrients in Indian diets, protein, calcium, iron and B-complex vitamins. Cereals contain 6-12 per cent protein which is generally deficient in lysine and provides more than 50 per cent of daily protein intake. Among cereals, rice protein is of better quality than the others. However, cereals when eaten with pulses, as is the common practice in India, the protein quality improves due to mutual supplementation between cereal and pulse proteins, the former being deficient while the latter being rich in lysine.

Cereals are also source of some nutrients like Ca and Fe. Although they are not rich in these minerals, they contribute significantly due to fairly large amounts of cereals consumed daily. However, rice among the cereals is poorer in these two minerals, the content depending upon the extent of polishing. Hence diets based predominantly on rice have lower Ca and Fe content. Ragi is rich in minerals, especially calcium. Millets including ragi are rich in minerals and fibre.

Inclusion of some amount of millets in a diet will help in making up deficiency of some of these minerals in the diet and in providing bulk (fibre) to diet, especially the rice based ones. It must be pointed out that these millets are also rich in phytate and tannin and hence interfere with mineral availability. A balance has to be struck between the positive and negative aspects of nutritional quality of millets.

Cereals, particularly the whole grains are an important source of B-vitamins in our diet. Since most of these vitamins reside in outer bran or polishing refining these grains (removal of bran) or polishing rice reduces B-vitamin content to different degrees depending upon the extent of refining and polishing. Highly polished rice has therefore very low level of B-vitamins. Parboiling which includes soaking in water and steaming of paddy results in seeping of vitamins present in outer layer into the grain. Hence milled and polished parboiled rice retains much of the vitamins. Same considerations apply to high extraction wheat flour (viz. maida) and pearled millets.

Cereals do not contain either vitamin A or vitamin C except that yellow maize and some varieties of sorghum contain small amount of β carotene.

Cereals are generally considered to have low fat content as determined by either extraction, which represents only the free fat. Recent studies however have shown that cereals contain much more fat, if the bound fat is also taken into account. The total fat including bound and free fat can be determined by hydrolysis with HCl followed by chloroform methanol extraction. The total fat content thus determined in cereals may vary from 2 to 5 per 100 g. considering the amount of cereals consumed it is estimated that fat present in cereals in our diets can meet more than 50 per cent of our essential fatty acid requirement. Cereals together with pulses can nearly meet the EFA requirement of an adult. Pulses (or legumes as they are also called) are rich source of protein in our diets. In a vegetarian diet or a diet containing low amounts of animal foods, they are an important source of protein. The major pulses which find an important place in our dietaries are tur (Arhar), bengalgram, blackgram, greengram, lentil. Some of them (bengalgram, greengram) are used as whole gram also. Others which are used as whole are cowpea, fieldbean, rajma. In amounts used, pulses and legumes do not contribute much to the total mineral intake. However, being rich in B-vitamins they can contribute significantly to B-vitamin intake. Like cereals they do not contain any vitamin A or vitamin C but germinated legumes contain some vitamin C.

The protein of pulses/legumes are of low quality since they are deficient in methionine and red gram is deficient in tryptophane also. However, they are rich in lysine. Hence they can supplement proteins of cereals and the quality of the protein from a mixture of cereals and pulses is superior to that of the either one. The most effective combination to achieve maximum supplementary effect is 4 parts of cereal protein + 1 part of pulse protein. In terms of the grains it will be 8 parts of cereals and 1 part of pulses.

Pulses with their higher content of total fat (visible + invisible) contribute along with cereals to meet the EFA needs of an adult. Many types of greens are consumed all over our country. The commonly consumed greens are palak, amaranth, fenugreek, drumstick, mint, etc. The green leafy vegetables are rich source of calcium, iron and β-carotene and vitamin C, riboflavin and folic acid. These greens are inexpensive and it is advisable to include at least 50 g of GLV daily in one's diet. They contain all important nutrients required for growth and maintenance of health. Hence GLV must be consumed by children, pregnant and nursing women to obtain much needed β-carotene, calcium and iron. This is particularly so on a predominantly cereal based diets of the poor who suffer from the dietary deficiency of these nutrients. Hence steps must be taken to encourage cultivation of GLV in kitchen gardens and school gardens so that they are available all through the year. Use of green leaves from trees like drumstick agathi, etc. helps to obtain them regularly without much effort if a tree is planted in a backyard.

Some of the important root vegetables which are commonly consumed in our country are tapioca, potato, sweet potato, carrots, yarm, colocacia. They are all rich in carbohydrate and can form an important source of energy in our diets. Carrots and yellow varieties of yam are rich in contene and potato is a significant source of vitamin C. Tapioca and yams are rich in calcium. Tapioca consumed in Kerala as energy source helps to meet a short supply in cereals during drought conditions.

Vegetables which do not come under green leafy vegetables and roots and tubers are classified under this head. This food group includes, several commonly used vegetables like brinjal, ladies fingers, French beans, guar beans, various gourds, tomatoes, etc. They not only add variety to the diet but also provide vitamin C and some minerals. These vegetables are also a source of dietary fibre in the diet and provide bulk to the diet.

Fruits are generally good sources of vitamin C. Amla and guava are the rich sources of this vitamin. Yellow fruits like mango and papaya in addition contain β-carotene, a precursor of vitamin A. The commonly used banana is a good source of carbohydrates and hence energy. Dried fruits are good source of iron. Fruits also contain pectins which provide bulk to the diet and helps bowel movement. Seasonal fruits must be included in the diet to supply vitamin C and β-carotene.

Another group covers liquid milk, milk powder, fermented products like curds, butter milk, etc. milk has always been considered an ideal food for infants and children and a good supplementary food for adults. Milk is not only a source of good quality protein, but also of calcium and riboflavin besides some other nutrients. Milk is however deficient in iron and vitamin C. Although milk from different species has similar nutritional value, there are some differences in the composition between human and cow's milk. human milk has less protein than cow's milk, the difference is mainly due to lower content of casein in human milk. Human milk also has higher lactose content as compared to cow's milk. Between cow's and buffalo milk, the latter has a higher content of fat expressed on moisture free basis. Unless the whey is discarded the products of milk retain all the nutrients present in the milk. However skimmed milk powder has no fat but has a higher level of protein and sugar on a moisture free basis.

Milk should find a place in any balanced diet particularly in a vegetarian diet, to provide some good quality protein, sufficient calcium and riboflavin which are difficult to obtain in adequate quantities solely from plant foods. An adult diet should have at least 150 ml of milk a day while children, pregnant and lactating women should receive at least 250 ml milk a day. Although milk production in our country has increased in the past decade or so, per capita availability still remains at 140 ml/day. The average consumption of milk in rural areas is around 70 ml per c.u. Among urban middle class it is around 250 ml. Vigorous efforts must be made to further increase milk availability in the country at least to meet the minimum nutrition goals. Under the existing conditions, efforts must be made to channelize the available milk to the vulnerable groups like young infants, preschool children, pregnant and lactating women. Bold policy decisions are required in this regard.

The visible fats commonly consumed in India are, butter, ghee, hydrogenated oils and various vegetable oils like groundnut oil, safflower.

Sugar and jaggery are sweetening agents in beverages and other foods to increase palatability. They essentially supply energy. Jaggery may contain some iron. Excessive consumption of refined sugar must be avoided as it may lead to heart diseases in adults and carries in children.

Flesh foods like meat, poultry and fish are rich in good quality proteins and they also provide B-vitamin. A special feature of flesh foods is their content of B_{12} which is absent in plant foods. Flesh foods are also source of vitamin A (liver). Fish is a good source of calcium. Fish also contain W-3 fatty (polyunsaturated) acids which are known to protect against cardiovascular diseases. Animal food production in our country is very low. Since some amount of animal food is useful in improving the quality of vegetarian diet, all efforts should be made to increase production of fish for which there is a good potential in our country and make it available to all segments of population which can consume it. Fish can be a substitute for pulses in cereal based diets of the poor.

There are accessory foods mainly used for flavouring food preparation to improve their palatability. These are used in small amounts and their contribution to nutrient intake is very limited. Some of these spices however are rich in iron, trace metals and potassium. Some of the condiments like chillies and coriander may provide some β-carotene. Green chillies provide β-carotene and vitamin C. Most of the spices contain a high level of tannin (viz. turmeric) which may interfere with iron absorption. These spices also contain several pharmacologically active substances like choline, biogenic amines, etc. Some of them like asopheotida and garlic have antibacterial property and inhibit putrifying bacteria.

Salt is also an important additive to our diets. Salt is used in our country is mostly sea salt and do not contribute anything but NaCl. Salt intake in our country is around 15 g per caput/day which may appear on the higher side. High salt intakes are associated with hypertension. It is possible in a tropical country like India where there may be excessive loss of Na through sweat, high level of NaCl is needed. But exact requirement of sodium by our people is not known. Sodium derived from foods is not significant. But potassium required by the body is primarily derived from food. A proper ratio of sodium to potassium intakes should be maintained to satisfy electrolyte balance and avoid undesirable consequence of excessive sodium.

Table 5.19. Nutrients intake by both rural and urban women

Nutrient intake	Rural			Urban			Z
	Mean ± SD	RDA	Deficit/ Increase (%)	Mean ± SD	RDA	Deficit/ Increase (%)	
Energy (Kcal)	3669±211	3233	+13.5	2301±196	2525	-8.9	49.820**
Protein (g)	60±16	65	-7.7	77±24	65	+18.5	6.181*
Fat (g)	37±9	30	+2.3	24±6	30	-20.0	12.605**
Iron (mg)	43±11	38	+13.1	46±13	38	+21.0	1.848
Calcium (mg)	1164±314	1000	+16.4	1281±367	1000	+28.1	2.541*
Carotene (µg)	2386±213	2400	-0.6	2406±303	2400	+0.2	0.566
Copper (mg)	2.9±0.1	3	-3.3	3.1±0.2	3	+3.3	9.381**
Manganese (mg)	408±38	450	-9.3	441±46	450	-2.0	5.801*
Zinc (mg)	29±5	30	-3.3	28±7	30	-6.7	1.219

The mean intake of nutrients by rural and urban pregnant women is presented in Table 5.19. Average energy intake by pregnant women of rural area was found 3669+211 Kcal per day and 2301+196 Kcal was found in urban pregnant women, value as compared to RDA was 13.5 per cent more in rural area and 8.9 per cent less in urban area.

According to expert group of planning commission, nutritional norm per capita daily intake of 2400 Kcal in urban area population were come in below poverty line. So on the basis of this both area population were come in below poverty line. The major source of energy for both group (rural and urban) was cereal. Devi and Vijaylakshmi (1976) stated that diet consumed by the expectant women of low income group was deficit in all nutrients and percentage deficit range from 8 to 63 per cent. Poor intake of energy have greater effect on birth weight of infants and more chances of pre mature delivery (Leela Raman, 1999).

Consumption of protein ranged between 45 and 65 g per day with an average of 60+16 for rural pregnant women and 50 to 70 g per day with an average of 77+24 g per day in urban area. By mean intake of protein in rural area failed to meet their RDA for protein i.e. 65 g per day (ICMR, 1989). Protein consumption was thus low in quantity. Most of the protein was derived from plant foods. It may be concluded that diet of both area women was low in energy and protein. Energy malnutrition during gestation was found to affect the brain development of foetus by limiting its structural and functional capabilities as well as performance (Gesh, 1980). Low intake of protein through diet lead to fail in providing excessive nitrogen and amino acid required for maternal and fetal tissue synthesis, lower concentration of amino acid have adverse effect on outcome (Kramer, 1987). Protein energy malnutrition may be associated with micronutrients malabsorption and interfere with iodide uptake by the thyroid (Gaitan *et al.,* 1983).

Fat included in the diet was visible as well as invisible, the average daily fat intake was 37+9 g per day in rural pregnant women and 24+6 g per day in urban pregnant women. The mean intake of fat was more in rural area and 20.0 per cent less in urban area i.e. rural and urban pregnant women as compared to recommended amount of 30 g per day. Gopalan (2002) reported that average total accretion of essential fatty acid during normal pregnancy of well nourished women could amount of 600 g. Nutritional consideration based on fat for Indian pregnant women showed a higher levels of requirement of 12.5 per cent from invisible fat through essential fatty acid. Deficiency of essential fatty acid during this period is believed to contribute poor vascular growth and subsequent rupture and coagulation in blood vessels leading to infraction in placenta (Winick, 1983).

Iron the most important element for the formation of haemoglobin of red blood cells of bloods. It's deficiency causes nutritional anaemia. Recommended dietary allowances for iron is 38 mg per day for pregnant women for meeting expansion of blood volume and growth of foetus.

It was found that daily average intake of iron 43+11 in rural women and 46+13 in urban pregnant women, on the basis of daily intake of iron it was found that both group women were anemic. Women of urban area may take iron and folic acid tablets but women of rural area i.e. 10 per cent may take iron folic acid tablets provided by ICDS and PHC. Gupta (1994) stated that prevalence of anemia among all women of low income group was 93.8 per cent and all the subjects were found to be deficient in iron and a positive correlation was found between iron intake and haemoglobin level. Iron deficiency anaemia is highly prevalent in women of developing countries and increased iron requirement are not often met by pregnant women through changes in diet and absorption (Beard, 2000).

Calcium and magnesium are both present in the diet and the body at levels much higher than those of other minerals such as iron. Approximately 99 per cent of the calcium and magnesium in the human body is located in the skeleton.

Pregnancy is a time for increased calcium demand because, the developing foetus, by term will have deposited 30 g of calcium in its own skeleton, most of this deposition occurring in the last 10 weeks of gestation. It is also important for neuromuscular function and blood coagulation factor in the foetus. Several changes in calcium metabolism associated with pregnancy facilitate the transfer of calcium from mother foetus while protecting calcium levels in maternal serum and bone. These include changes in calcium regulating hormones, which affect intestinal absorption, renal reabsorption and bone turnover of calcium. Increased intestinal absorption are mediated by increased levels of vitamin D (1,23-$(0H)_2$D). Parathyroid hormone (PTH) stimulates bone resorption by activating oteocytic osteolysis, facilitates intestinal absorption (by increasing the synthesis of vitamin D) and interferes with tubular reabsorption. Total serum calcium decreases gradually throughout pregnancy. This is associated with and parallels the drop in serum albumin (to which 60% of the serum calcium is attached) that results from expansion of the extra cellular fluid volume. However these changes are not wide and remain within normal range.

Concern over calcium intake during pregnancy gained much importance, when it appeared that as much as 10 g of net bone loss occur during normal pregnancy. Additionally, several reports have suggested an increased incidence of blood pressure in those with low dietary calcium irrespective of energy and protein intake. The best example which can be cited here is that of poor urban and rural Guatemalan pregnant women, whose energy intake is marginal (100 cals/d) have lowest incidence (0.4%) of eclampsia in the world against the developed countries like Japan whose incidence of eclampsia is very high. The calcium intake was 110 mg/d in Guatemalan pregnant women whereas Japanese were taking about 368 mg of calcium/d. Thus considering the blood pressure lowering effect of calcium, several studies conducted successful supplemental trials, which resulted not only in improved blood pressure, low incidence of eclampsia and pregnancy induced hypertension (PIH), but also improved birth weight, lactational performance and low incidence of pre-term delivery. Thus when considering the calcium status, dietary calcium should be taken into account rather than serum/plasma calcium levels.

Average daily intake of calcium was 1164+314 in rural pregnant women and 1281+367 in urban pregnant women with the range of 840 mg to 1200 mg for rural and 840 mg to 1350 mg for urban. Average intake of calcium was inadequate for both groups when compared to recommended dietary allowance of 1000 mg per day (ICMR, 1989). Urban pregnant women consuming higher amount of calcium per day because they take milk properly in their diet.

β-arotene is essential for normal vision, maintaining integrity of epithelial tissue and a wide variety of metabolic function. β-carotene is converted to retinal in the body before utilization (Khanna *et al.*, 1997) the ICMR expert committee recommended a daily allowance of 600 μg of retinal for both adult man and women including pregnant women also. In terms of β-carotene this work out to be 2400 μg per day, in view of incomplete absorption and inefficient conversion of β-carotene to retinol. Average daily intake of β-carotene was 2386+213 in rural area and in urban area 2406+303. The percentage deficit of carotene range from 0.6 per cent in rural area and 0.2 per cent more in urban area. Vitamin A deficiency during gestation can lead to fetal wastage (Azais-Braesco and Pasca, 2000). It may lead to complication of pregnancy and abnormal fetal development. The striking finding related to supplementation of β-carotene indicate that weekly vitamin A or β-carotene supplements reduced maternal mortality by 50 per cent controlled trial in Nepal (West *et al.*, 1999).

Copper and zinc were the most investigated elements during past 20 years. Copper is widely distributed in biological tissues and largely occurs in organic complexes, many of which are metalloproteins and function as enzymes. Copper containing enzymes are involved in a variety of metabolic reactions, such as utilization of oxygen during cell respiration and energy utilization. They are also involved in the synthesis of essential tissues of the skeleton and blood vessels and in a range of neuro active compounds concerned in nervous tissue functions. Certain cuproenzymes like superoxide dismutase in cytosol or mitochondria are important in the body's defense against free radicals. Though copper deficiency has not been documented in human pregnancy, as early as in 1969 interesting revelations were made by Friedman *et al.* (1969). They reported abnormally high serum copper values in pre-eclampsia and low values as an indication for placental insufficiency and impending fetal health. Serum copper has been reported to be lower in women who has premature deliveries. Weak correlations were observed between maternal serum copper, hair copper and fetal growth and also in conditions like PIH 2 eclampsia, pregnancy has a major effect on maternal copper metabolism. Serum copper levels increase progressively during gestation, reaching to 2 to 2.5 times higher than non-pregnant levels, near terms. This significant rise in copper level is due to the increased plasma levels of ceruloplasmin (an $á_2$–globulin) to which binds over 90 per cent of the serum copper. This rise in ceruloplasmin concentration is believed to be influenced by the increasing estrogen levels during pregnancy.

Though the average intake of copper is reported to be 1 mg/day against 2.2 mg/day RDA, copper deficiency per se has not been reported in humans (due to low dietary copper). Also copper intake did not showed any correlations to pregnancy outcome such as birth weight. However, serum copper levels appears to be of significant value in assessing the copper status as well as risk to the pregnancy, but it still remain to be elucidated further.

The average intake of copper was 2.9+0.1 mg per day in rural women and 3.1+0.2 mg per day in urban pregnant women. The percentage deficit 3.3 per cent in rural pregnant women and 3.3 per cent more in urban women when compared with recommended dietary allowance of 3.0 mg per day. All trace element are associated with pregnancy complication and copper deficiency may be associated with adverse outcome of pregnancy and reduced fetal growth (Arnaud *et al.*, 1994). Basically in body it act as an enzyme, copper containing enzymes are involved in variety of metabolic function specially in utilization of O_2 and cell respiration (Umamaheshwari, 1997). High serum copper values resulting in pre eclampsia and low value as an indication of placental.

Magnesium is an essential mineral and appears to participate in more than 300 enzymatic reactions in the body. It is essential in cyclic adenosine monophosphate dependent membrane transport, glycolysis and even in genetic transcription and translation. The metabolism of magnesium is not regulated by any known hormones. The maternal serum magnesium concentration rises slightly in early pregnancy, returning to non-pregnant levels by late pregnancy. Patients with pregnancy induced hypertension and eclampsia were found to be having significant lower plasma magnesium levels as compared to the normal pregnant women of some gestational age.

The role of magnesium in improving perinatal outcome is still unclear. The use of magnesium sulphate as a tocolytic and seizure prophylactic in pre-eclampsia has led to the hypothesis that antepartum magnesium supplementation could have beneficial effect on perinatal outcome. Many studies reported lower incidence of low birth weight, premature births, fever hospitalization of the neonates to intensive care units in supplemented groups. Considering the wide distribution of magnesium in nature nutritional deficiency appears to be rare, though magnesium deficiency has been implicated in states of malnutrition, uncontrolled diabetes during pregnancy and pregnancy induced hypertension (PIH).

Thus, though some of the studies revealed positive outcome of pregnancy with increased magnesium intake, detailed studies are yet to be done to confirm on its supplementation. However serum magnesium levels appears to be of some value in finding out its status in eclamptic and PIH conditions.

Average daily intake of manganese was 408+38 in rural pregnant women and 441+46 was in urban pregnant women. The percentage deficit range in rural pregnant was 9.3 per cent and 2.0 per cent in urban women as compared to RDA value i.e. 450 mg per day. Manganese is an essential element as it participates in a number of reaction as a co-enzyme. Diets of poor income have better absorption as compared to diets of high income group (Gopalan, 1999). Manganese deficiency is not likely to occur in Indian population.

Zinc an important element for normal reproduction and also for growth and development at molecular level. The average intake of zinc was 8.5+2.9 in rural population and 11.6+4.0 mg per day in urban areas. The percentage deficit range for rural pregnant women was 35 per cent and 25.4 per cent in urban pregnant women. The recommended dietary allowance for zinc is 15.5 mg per day for every group. Iron supplement can interfere with the absorption of zinc and zinc in high doses interfere with the absorption of copper and iron (Soloman and Ruz, 1997). So these micro nutrients have negative interaction in humans. So these micro-nutrients have negative interaction in humans. Randomized control trials of zinc supplementation have largely done in developed country trials found benefits in reduction of low birth weight and pre terms delivery (Jameson, 1982).

There is little evidence for effects on fetal birth weight despite widespread deficiency of vitamin A. Low serum levels or vitamin 'C' or low intake (<20 mg/day) is associated with increased risk of preterm birth. 60–70 per cent of pregnant women has folate levels <125 ng/ml RBC's. Since folate is closely involved in the growth and multiplications of cells, folate deficiency has an adverse impact on the fetal outcome.

Fetal growth retardation can result from maternal megaloblastic anaemia. Supplementation at least for 100 days during pregnancy results in improvement of mean birth weight by 200 g. The incidence of LBW decreased by 50 per cent with daily supplementation of 500 mg of folate. Thiamine deficiency can results in an increased incidence of infantile beri-beri even when there are no clinical signs of deficiency in the mothers. Pernicious anaemia, even though is rare, low biochemical measures of vitamin B_{12} is observed in early life among infants of women who had followed vegan (no animal protein) diets for an extended period. Reduced bone density, neonatal hypocalcaemia and fetal rickets have been associated with maternal deficiencies of vitamin D and calcium, usually because of deficient diet combined with lack of exposure to sunlight.

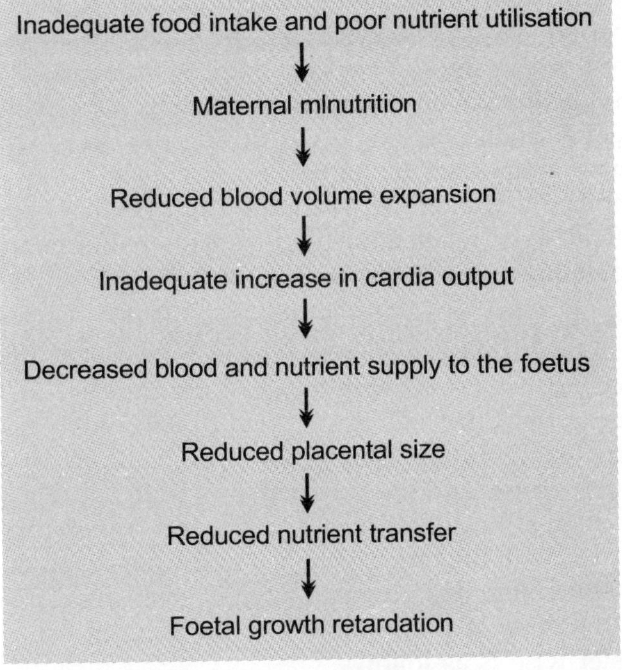

Relationship between maternal and foetal nutrition

Table 5.20. Nutrients intake by pregnant women in trimester

Trimester	Rural		Urban	
	Normal	Low	Normal	Low
First	81 (73.6)	29 (26.4)	92 (83.6)	18 (16.4)
Second	73 (66.4)	37 (33.6)	86 (78.2)	24 (21.8)
Third	64 (58.2)	46 (41.8)	78 (70.9)	32 (29.1)

Table 5.20 shows the nutrients intake by pregnant women in trimester. Pregnancy may be considered in three stages. The first 2 weeks following conceptions the fertilized ovum becomes implanted in the endometrium of the uterus and rapid cell proliferation occurs. Initially the uterine glands and the outer layers of the germ plasm nourish the embryo and the placenta begins to develop.

About 2 to 8 weeks, all the major organs are formed during this period—heart, kidneys, lungs, liver, and skeleton. At the end of 8 weeks the embryo is about 2.5 cm long and weighs about 4 g. Studies on experimental animals have shown that congenital malformations occur during this stage when the pregnant animal has had a diet grossly deficient in vitamin A, riboflavin, vitamin B_6, vitamin B_{12} or folacin. However, it is difficult to correlate these findings with malformations that are sometimes seen in human infants.

Eighth week to term, rapid growth of the foetus occurs. Most of the increase in length of the foetus takes place during the second trimester, while most of the increase in weight occurs in the third trimester. Also during this period the maternal reserves are established in preparation for labour, the puerperium, and the production of milk. During each of these stages, both cell hyperplasia and hypertrophy are occurring, with the rate of each varying from organ to organ. The requirement of a pregnant woman is mostly increased in the latter half of pregnancy. The increase in calories for trimester-wise is as follows :

1st trimester — 10 cals/day

2nd trimester — 90 cals/day

3rd trimester — 200 cals/day

Any decrease in the activity of the mother decreases the caloric requirement. It is very evident that normal pregnancy calls for a considerable weight gain over and above that represented by the size of the foetus. The fat that accumulates throughout pregnancy (specially for the first 30 weeks) acts as an energy reserve. When the supply of calories are inadequate the fat may be used up to provide the high energy needs of the rapidly growing foetus and to spare the proteins for tissue growth. This results in an increase in the ketones in the urine during the 1st trimester of pregnancy. The foetus does not accumulate any fat except in the cell walls and system. All the fat is synthesised from glucose except for the only essential fatty acid (linoleic acid) which is transferred from the mother to the child.

Zinc is an essential element for normal human reproduction, growth, development and life span. At the molecular levels, zinc is involved extensively in nucleic acid and protein metabolism and, hence, in the fundamental processes of cell differentiation and replication. Zinc and zinc-dependent enzymes for example, or involved in the synthesis of deoxyribonucleic acid (DNA), ribonucleic acid (RNA), and ribosomes. Zinc deficiency reduces the activity of these enzymes, but disturbances of all replication and differentiation appear to be attributable primarily to the adverse effects of zinc deficiency on gene expression. Fore example, zinc fingers play a critical role in the attachment of the transcription proteins to DNA. These fingers are projections, the shape of which is dependent on a zinc atom at the base. This essential step is the initiation of the transcription process is but one example of the numerous ways in which zinc is involved in all stages of the cell cycle. Thus, it is not surprising that low zinc status is associated with intrauterine growth retardation

(IUGR), neural tube defects, specifically in encephaly and spinobifida.

Circulating levels of maternal zinc provide an index of zinc provide an index of zinc utilization during pregnancy. By late pregnancy the concentration of circulating zinc is 15-35 per cent lower than valves in non pregnant women. The decline occurs as early as the first gestational month and appears to stabilize during the second trimester. However, several investigators have reported another gradual decline in circulating zinc after the second trimester and was attributed to fetal uptake. The mechanisms responsible for the decline in maternal zinc values remain speculative. Several factors may be involved. Similar to other nutrients, an important component of the decline would be plasma volume expansion. Plasma zinc is mostly bound to albumin. Since plasma albumin concentration decreases in pregnancy, this may account for some of the decline in plasma zinc levels. During gestation the affinity of the albumin molecules of zinc is somewhat decreased resulting in increased urinary excretion of zinc.

Usual daily dietary zinc intakes during pregnancy ranged form 8.8 to 14.4 mg/d against the RDA of 15.5 mg/d. Among vegetarians and low socio-economic groups this intake appears to be even lower. Low socio-economic groups of pregnant women when supplemented with daily zinc of 20 mg/d, their serum zinc levels improved significantly. Yet another study revealed pregnant women having less than 50 mg/dl of serum zinc, suffered from conditions like pregnancy induced hypertension and eclampsia and these pregnant women gave birth to low birth weight infants. Thus, low dietary zinc as well as low serum zinc levels appear to be 'markers' for poor reproductive performance. However, results of supplementation studies are equivocal, therefore, this area of improving zinc status through supplementation further exulted by double-blind randomized clinical trials.

Other trace minerals like chromium, iodine, manganese and selenium remains to be further explored. Considering the wide spread deficiency of iodine is in our country, distribution of iodised salt is in operation. The only confirmed function of iodine is to constitute an essential substrate for the synthesis of thyroid hormone, tetraiodathyronie (thyroxine or T_4) and triiodothyronine (T_3). The thyroid hormones in turn, play a decisive role in the metabolism of all cells of the organisms and in the process of early growth and development of most organs, especially of the brain. Brain development in humans occurs from fetal life up to the third postnatal year. Consequently, a deficit in iodine and or in thyroid hormones occurring during this critical period of life will result not only in the slowing down of the metabolic activities of the organism but also irreversible alterations in the development of the brain.

Minerals though required in small amounts perform vital activities in the body. The effective concentrations of elements are very low and a delicate balance exists between toxicity, vitality and deficiency, because the distance between two extremes is uncomfortably close. Since the picture of role of minerals are still not complete or clear, new discoveries can be expected with the advent of latest analytical methods, though fundamental chemical roles are very well established for many minerals like calcium, zinc etc.

In first trimester 73.6 per cent rural women and 83.6 per cent urban pregnant women were more careful about nutrients intake and diet. Pregnancy is a period of great importance and interest in the life of every female. Completing the pregnancy uneventfully and having a normal healthy baby is the most rewarding aspect of it. Minerals are important both as structural and functional components in the body because of their essential role in cell metabolism. Pregnancy is a time for increased calcium demand because the developing foetus, by term will have deposited 30 g of calcium in its own skeleton and it is also important for neuromuscular function and blood coagulation factor in the foetus. Two thirds of foetal calcium is transferred from the mother to the foetus after 30th week of pregnancy at the rate of 300 mg per day. Dairy products are a primary source of calcium, green leafy vegetables also contribute to calcium. Magnesium is an essential mineral and appears to participate in more than 300 enzymatic reactions in the body. 66.4 per cent rural and 78.2 per cent urban pregnant women have taking normal nutrients in second trimester, zinc is an essential element for normal human reproduction, growth, development and life span. Circulating levels of maternal zinc provide an index of zinc utilization during pregnancy, late pregnancy the concentration of circulating zinc is 15-35 per cent lower than values in non-pregnant women. The decline occurs as early as the first gestational month and appears to stabilize during the second trimester. Copper is widely distributed in biological tissues and largely occurs in organic complexes, many of which are metalloproteins and function as enzymes. 58.2 per cent rural and 70.9 per cent urban pregnant women have taking normal diet in third trimester of pregnancy, normal iron requirement during pregnancy is 38 mg/day. The total iron requirement for the entire period of pregnancy is 810 mg. The actual increase in requirement of iron is only in second and third trimester. Green leafy vegetables, eggs and iron fortified salt provides additional sources of iron. The caloric requirements of a pregnant women were mostly increased in the latter half of pregnancy in 2nd trimester required 90 cals/day and 3rd trimester 200 cals/day. The normal protein requirement of an adult women is 50 g/day and for pregnant women 65 g/day. For pregnant women the requirement of thiamin is increased by 0.2 mg/day.

Table 5.21 indicates that pregnant women taking special food in diet, 89.1 per cent urban women were taking cereals, 90.9 per cent urban women taking milk, 83.6 per cent urban women taking green vegetables, 87.3 per cent women taking fruit and 82.7 per cent urban women taking jaggery according to doctor advise. Majority of rural pregnant women have taking advise by elder women in family for special food. Less

Table 5.21. Pregnant women taking special food in diet

Special food	Doctor advise		Elder women in family		Elder women outsider	
	Rural	Urban	Rural	Urban	Rural	Urban
Cereals	43 (39.1)	98 (89.1)	82 (74.5)	48 (43.6)	63 (57.3)	14 (12.7)
Milk	46 (41.8)	100 (90.9)	64 (58.2)	41 (37.3)	54 (49.1)	18 (16.4)
Green vegetable	39 (35.4)	92 (83.6)	56 (50.9)	46 (41.8)	51 (46.4)	20 (18.2)
Fruit	34 (30.9)	96 (87.3)	48 (43.6)	52 (47.3)	46 (41.8)	17 (15.4)
Jaggery	41 (37.3)	91 (82.7)	59 (53.6)	36 (32.7)	38 (34.5)	11 (10.0)

(Figures in parenthesis indicate percentage of respective values)

majority of rural women were taking advise of doctor for taking special food in diet. About 50.0 per cent rural women were taking advise of elder women outsider for special food in diet in pregnancy period. The requirements of special food in pregnancy was based upon the cereals, milk, green vegetable and jaggery arising out of the growth of maternal tissues. Mothers who are residing in goiter endemic areas should ensure that they get enough iodine through iodised salt and other means lever, egg yolk, butter, dark green and yellow vegetables and fruits are good source of vitamin A. Dairy milk products are a primary source of calcium. Dried fruits, green leafy vegetables, eggs and enriched cereals and iron fertified salt product additional sources of iron. Milk, meat, egg and cheese are complete proteins and of high biological value. Additional protein may be obtained from legumes and whole grains, nuts and oilseeds.

Table 5.22. Pregnant women according to avoided food

Avoided food	Rural		Urban		χ^2
	Yes	No	Yes	No	
Papaya	91 (82.7)	19 (17.3)	86 (78.2)	24 (21.8)	0.723
Ginger	79 (71.8)	31 (28.2)	66 (60.0)	44 (40.0)	3.419*
Tamarind	76 (69.1)	34 (30.9)	82 (74.5)	28 (25.5)	0.808
High dose medicine	93 (84.5)	17 (15.5)	60 (54.5)	50 (45.5)	23.371*

(Figures in parenthesis indicate percentage of respective values)

The perusal of Table 5.22 reveals that pregnant women according to avoided food, 82.7 per cent rural pregnant women and 78.2 per cent urban pregnant women were avoiding papaya in the diet whereas 71.8 per cent rural women and 60.0 per cent urban women were not taking ginger in a diet. 69.1 per cent rural women and 74.5 per cent urban women were not taking tamarind while 84.5 per cent rural women and 54.5 per cent urban women were not taking high dose medicine during pregnancy period. In urban environment about 50.0 per cent women have taking medicine in pregnancy period, the observed value of χ^2 (23.371**) was significant at 1 per cent level of significance.

The use of drugs during pregnancy and pureperium is a question of time balance. No harm should be allowed to be all on the baby because of the drug. At the same time no harm should be must come to the mother or baby because of a disease that is being inadequately treated. Information about the safe and effective use of drugs in pregnancy has not kept pace with the advances in other areas of therapeutics.

The birth of infant is the expectation of parents when pregnancy is considered. Normality is not limited to the time of birth, but includes the achievement of full potential in adulthood. Today advances in medical knowledge and delivery have made this aspiration more readily available than ever before.

However, there is a threat to the fulfillment of the prospective parents dreams resulting from the very advances that contributed to better health.

Indeed modern technology poses a risk to the foetus and lactating infant from the drugs used in obstetric practice and from the increasing number of chemicals in the environment. New social cultural and ecologic conditions have modified the experience of today's pregnant women. Studies are needed to clarify their specific impact and facilitate the development of preventive and/or curative strategies.

The use of drugs during pregnancy and in the pyerperium requires that a fine balance should be maintained. Such as amiodarone, asprin, barbiturates, benzodiazepines, contraceptives, cytotoxic drugs, tetracycline's ephedrine.

Table 5.23 shows that problems faced by pregnant women, 60.0 per cent rural women and 86.4 per cent urban pregnant women were faced nausea and vomiting may be due to nervous disturbances, placental protein intoxication or due to derangement in carbohydrate metabolism. Condition

Table 5.23. Distribution of pregnant women as per problems

Problems	Rural	Urban	X^2
Nausea and vomiting	66 (60.0)	95 (86.4)	19.478**
Constipation	54 (49.1)	85 (77.3)	17.497**
Oedema and leg cramps	36 (32.7)	92 (83.6)	58.587**
Heartburn	12 (10.9)	46 (41.8)	27.067**
Beliefs, avoidances, cravings and aversions	44 (40.0)	67 (60.9)	9.619**
Weight gain during pregnancy	85 (77.3)	96 (87.3)	3.771*

(Figures in parenthesis indicate percentage of respective values)

develop to hyperemesis gravidarum, a severe prolonged persistent vomiting, peripheral parenteral nutrition. 49.1 per cent rural women and 77.3 per cent urban pregnant women have faced constipation, the pressure of the enlarging uterus on the lower portion of the intestine in addition to the hormonal muscle relaxant effect of placental hormones on the gastrointestinal tract and physical inactivity may make elimination difficult. Increased fluid intake, vegetables rich fibre and juices induce regularly for proper elimination. 32.7 per cent rural women and 83.6 per cent urban women have faced oedema and leg cramps, mild physiologic oedema is usually present in the extremities in the third trimester. Normal oedema requires no sodium restriction or other dietary changes. The common occurrence of cramps during pregnancy, manifested nocturnally by sudden contractions of the muscle, is thought to be related to a decline in serum calcium levels related to a calcium phosphorus imbalance. Heart burn is a common complaint during the latter part of pregnancy in 41.8 per cent urban women were faced this is an effect of pressure of the enlarged uterus on the stomach which in combination with the relaxation of the oesophageal sphincter. 40.0 per cent rural women and 60.9 per cent urban women respondents have suffered beliefs, avoidances,

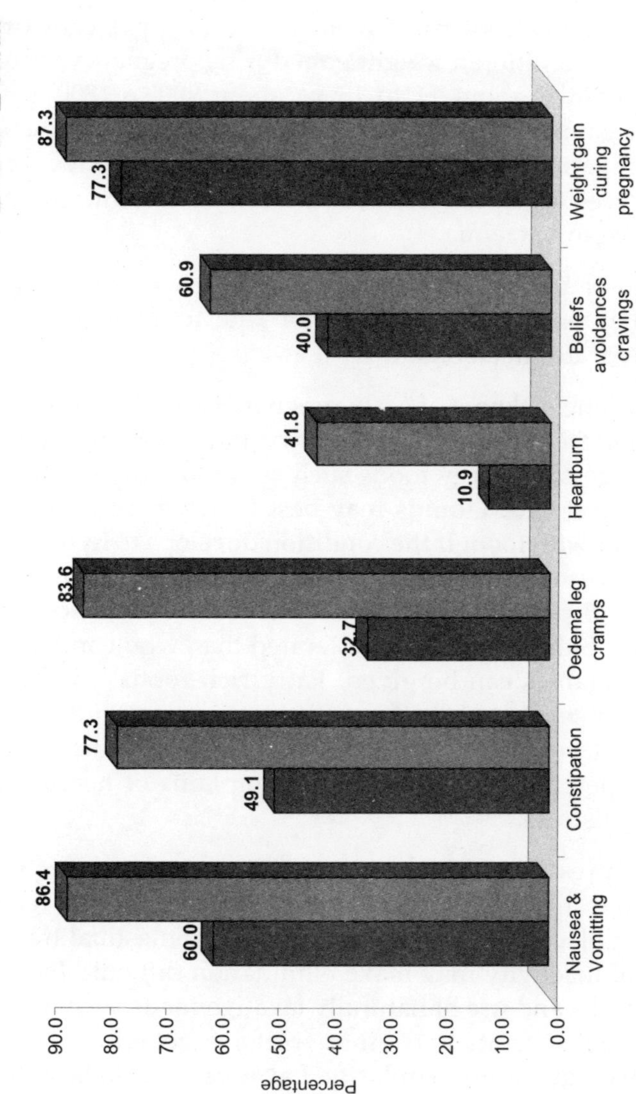

Fig. 5.10 : Distribution of pregnant women as per problems

cravings and aversions urges toward or away foods which women experience no unusual attitudes but aversions reported are to alcohol, coffee, meal and strongly spiced foods. 77.3 per cent rural women and 87.3 per cent urban women have suffered weight gain during pregnancy, optimal weight gain is about 11 to 13 kg about 900 to 1800 g is an average gain during the first trimester. Sharp sudden increase in weight after the 20th week of pregnancy. Excessive weight gain places an extra strain on the organs and increases the incidence to toxaemia.

Nausea in pregnancy may be due to nervous disturbances, placental protein intoxication or due to derangement in carbohydrate metabolism.

Morning sickness of early pregnancy can be improved by small and frequent meals. Fairly dry and consisting chiefly of easily digested energy foods such as carbohydrates are more readily tolerated. Liquids may best be taken between meals instead of with food. If the condition develops to hyperemesis gravidarum, a severe prolonged persistent vomiting, peripheral parenteral nutrition and careful oral feeding is essential. Skin milk is better tolerated than whole milk. Fruits and vegetables can be given. Fatty rich foods, fried foods, excessive seasoning, coffee in large amounts and strongly flavoured vegetables may be restricted or eliminated if the nausea persists or if the patient complains of heartburn or gastric distress.

The pressure of the enlarging uterus on the lower portion of the intestine, in addition to the hormonal muscle relaxant effect of placental hormones on the gastrointestinal tract and physical inactivity may make elimination difficult. Increased fluid intake and use of naturally laxative foods such as whole grains, dried fruits and other fruits, vegetables rich fibre, juices usually induce regularity, Laxatives should be avoided. Regular habits of exercise and sleep are essential for proper elimination.

Mild physiologic oedema is usually present in the extremities in the third trimester. The swelling of the lower extremities may be caused by the pressure of the enlarging uterus on the veins returning fluid from the legs. This normal oedema requires no sodium restriction or other dietary changes.

The common occurrence of cramps during pregnancy, manifested nocturnally by sudden contractions of the muscle, is thought to be related to a decline in serum calcium levels related to a calcium phosphorus imbalance. Prevention or relief of these leg cramps has been reported with reduction of milk (a high phosphorus, high calcium beverage) intake and supplementation with non-phosphate calcium salts. Magnesium is another mineral with the potential for relieving leg cramps.

Heartburn is a common complain during the latter part of pregnancy. In most cases, this is an effect of pressure of the enlarged uterus on the stomach which in combination with the relaxation of the oesophageal sphincter, results in occasional regurgitation of the stomach contents into the esophagus. This can usually be relieved by limiting the amount of food consumed at one time and drinking fluids between meals. Sitting upright after meals for at least 3 hours before lying down may also help.

Food avoidances reflect mother's conscious choice not to consume certain foods during pregnancy e.g., heat producing foods like papaya and gingelly seeds.

Craving and aversions are powerful urges toward or away form foods which women experience no unusual attitudes when not pregnant. The most commonly craved foods are sweets and dairy products. The most common aversions reported are to alcohol, coffee, other caffeinated drinks, meats and strongly spiced foods.

Consumption of non-food items like laundry starch, ice cubes or clay is called pica. It occurs more often during pregnancy than at any other time. The etiology of pica is poorly understood one theory suggested that the ingestion of non-food substances relieves nausea and vomiting. It has also been hypothesized that a deficiency for essential nutrient such as calcium or iron, results in the eating of non-food substances that contain these nutrients. Much of this behaviour appears to be based on superstitions, customs and traditions that one often passes from mother to daughter.

Table 5.24. Complications during pregnancy faced by women

Compli-cations	Rural		Urban		χ^2
	Yes	No	Yes	No	
Anaemia	86 (78.2)	24 (21.8)	84 (76.4)	26 (23.6)	0.104
Hypertension disorders	35 (31.8)	75 (68.2)	76 (69.1)	34 (30.9)	30.566**
Urinary tract infection	76 (69.1)	34 (30.9)	67 (60.9)	43 (39.1)	1.618
Vaginal blee-ding in preg-nancy	88 (80.0)	22 (20.0)	85 (77.3)	25 (22.7)	0.243
Syphilis	78 (70.9)	32 (29.1)	37 (33.6)	73 (66.4)	30.627**
HIV/AIDS	2 (01.8)	108 (98.2)	14 (12.7)	96 (87.3)	9.706*
Malaria	27 (24.5)	83 (75.5)	4 (03.6)	106 (96.4)	19.863**
Intestinal parasite	46 (41.8)	64 (58.2)	16 (14.5)	94 (85.5)	20.212**

(Figures in parenthesis indicate percentage of respective values)

Table 5.24 shows that complications during pregnancy faced by respondents both rural and urban women were suffering by anaemia during pregnancy while 69.1 per cent urban women have faced hypertensive disorders. Urinary tract infection and vaginal bleeding in pregnancy have in both side of women (rural and urban) during pregnancy. 70.9 per cent rural women and 33.6 per cent urban women have syphilis during pregnancy, the observed value of χ^2 (30.627**) was significant at 1 per cent level of significance. 41.8 per cent rural women and 14.5 per cent urban women have faced

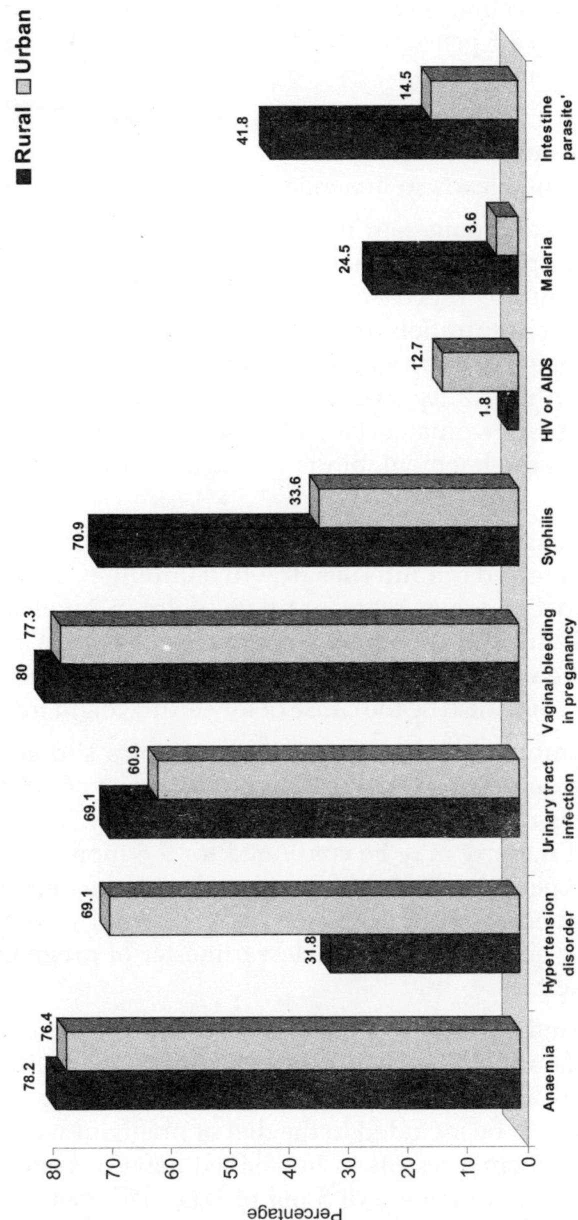

Fig. 5.11 : Complications during pregnancy faced by women

complication intestinal parasite whereas 24.5 per cent rural women and only 3.6 per cent urban women have faced malaria during pregnancy period.

Too little space between births or too many infections and too little intake of nutrients involved in erythroposis during pregnancy leads to anaemia.

Physiological changes in the blood occur progressively during normal pregnancy. Haemoglobin mass increases, red blood cell volume increases, plasma volume rises and haemoglobin concentration drops from 13.4 to 11.6 g per 100 ml. Severe anaemia in pregnant women increases maternal morbidity and mortality and involves a higher risk of the foetus. A pregnant woman is labeled anaemic if from the 28th week onwards the haemoglobin is less than 10 g per 100 ml of blood.

A significant fall in birth weight due to increase in prematurity rate and intrauterine growth retardation has been reported to occur when maternal haemoglobin level falls below 8 g/dl. Anaemic pregnant women are prone to urinary infections. The effect of anaemia and urinary tract infection in pregnancy could also be the cause of low birth weight infant.

The predominantly cereal diet in the tropics should be able to provide 40 mg iron per day. Treatment of highly deficient states requires daily therapeutic doses of 120 to 200 mg. This oral therapy may be continued for 3-6 months after anaemia has been corrected in order to replenish the depleted stores. Administration orally of 60 mg elemental iron and 500 μg of folic acid per day in the last trimester of pregnancy prevents anaemia.

The demand for folate is increased because of increased cellular proliferation. The low folate levels are due to deficient intake. Folates are easily destroyed by cooking, hence fresh vegetables should be included in the diet of pregnant woman. Megaloblastic anemia results in intensified nausea, vomiting and anorexia. A supplement of 5 mg of folic acid ensures an adequate supply for prophylactic purposes.

Anaemia duet o B_{12} deficiency in pregnancy is uncommon. A single injection of 40 mcg of B_{12} is enough to produce a maximum response in 10 days in B_{12} deficient mothers.

Studies conducted at National Institute of Nutrition (1992-93) indicate that severe pregnancy induced hypertension (eclampsia) are associated with higher incidence of vitamin A and protein deficiencies resulting in poor pregnancy outcome.

It is common among women subsisting on inadequate diets with little or no prenatal care. The symptoms of PIH include hypertension, abnormal and excessive oedema, albuminuria, convulsions or coma. Optimal nutrition is a fundamental aspect of therapy. Emphasis is given to adequate dietary protein. Correction of plasma protein deficits stimulates normal operation of the capillary fluid shift mechanism and circulation of fluid tissue with subsequent correction of the hypovolaemia (abnormal reduction in volume of circulatory plasma). In addition, adequate salt and sources of vitamins and minerals are needed for correction and maintenance of metabolic balance.

In severe pre-eclampsia, oral feeding is suspended in favour of intravenous infusion with 10 per cent dextrose drip during which the patient remains in sedation. Then oral feeding with 10 per cent dextrose, barley and fruit juice is allowed. Bed rest is advocated in that case.

This can cause considerable maternal and foetal consequences. Nutritional therapy will centre on: (*i*) prevention of weight extremes, underweight or obesity; (*ii*) correction of any dietary deficiencies and maintenance of optimal nutritional status during pregnancy; and (*iii*) management of any related preexisting disease such as diabetes mellitus. Sodium intake may be moderate but should not be unduly restricted.

During pregnancy glycosuria is not uncommon, because of the increased circulating blood volume and its load of metabolites. Most of these women revert to normal glucose tolerance after delivery.

Table 5.25. Consumption of food groups according to frequency

Frequency		> once day	One per day	3 to 6 time per week	1-2 times per week	1-2 times per month
GLVs	Rural	—	12 (19.9)	70 (63.6)	18 (16.4)	10 (09.1)
	Urban	9 (08.2)	32 (29.1)	23 (20.9)	38 (34.5)	8 (07.3)
Fruits	Rural	2 (01.8)	—	10 (09.1)	56 (50.9)	42 (38.2)
	Urban	18 (16.4)	59 (53.6)	17 (15.4)	10 (09.1)	6 (05.4)
Milk and milk products	Rural	6 (05.4)	8 (07.3)	41 (37.3)	17 (15.4)	38 (34.5)
	Urban	38 (34.5)	39 (35.4)	11 (10.0)	22 (20.0)	—
Nuts and Oilseeds	Rural	13 (11.8)	27 (24.5)	19 (17.3)	41 (37.3)	10 (09.1)
	Urban	20 (18.2)	21 (19.1)	39 (35.4)	28 (25.4)	2 (01.8)
Roots tuber and other	Rural	6 (05.4)	38 (34.5)	43 (39.1)	15 (13.6)	8 (07.3)
	Urban	3 (02.7)	16 (14.5)	8 (07.3)	50 (45.4)	33 (30.0)

Frequency of Consumption of Food Groups

Table 5.25 revealed that more than once per day frequency of consumption regarding fruits, green leafy vegetables (GLVs), nuts and oil seed and root and tuber were less percentage in rural areas whereas more per cent found in urban areas. Fruits were consume more in once a day and one per day 70.0 per cent urban pregnant women and 90.0 per cent rural pregnant women were consumed 1-2 times month and 1 to 2 times per week. 40 per cent rural pregnant women consume root and tuber once/day and 17.0 per cent urban women consume root tuber and other once/day. 35.0 per cent rural women were consume nuts and oilseed once a day whereas 37.3 per cent urban women were consume nuts and oilseeds.

Table 5.26. Moisture content of under-utilized leaves on fresh weight

S.No.	Plant species	Local name	Moisture (%)
1.	*Amaranthus spinous*	Chauli	89.3
2.	*Basella rubra*	Poi	96.5
3.	*Brassica campestris*	Sarson	90.2
4.	*Brassica oleracea*	Phool Gobhi leaves	89.8
5.	*Colocasia esculantum*	Arvi	87.2
6.	*Cicer arietinum*	Channa sag	77.8
7.	*Ipomea aquticafrask*	Nari, Kalmi, Karemua	90.9
8.	*Chenopodium album*	Bathua	93.4
9.	*Moringa oleifera*	Sahjan leaves	71.5
10.	*Spinacia oleracea*	Palak	88.2

Table 5.24 reveals that moisture content of under-utilized leaves on fresh weight, moisture content in leaves ranges from 71.4 per cent to 96.6 per cent maximum in *Basella rubra* followed by 93.3 per cent in *Chenopodium album,* 90.9 per cent in *Ipomea aqutica,* 90.2 per cent in *Brassica campestris* on fresh weight basis. 88.2 per cent moisture in *Spinacia oleracea* and 77.8 per cent moisture in Channa sag. Gopalan (1999) and Katiyar (1985)

reported same moisture content in these leaves. Generally moisture content in green leafy vegetable ranges from 80-90 per cent.

Table 5.27. Micro nutrient content of underutilized leaves on dry weight basis

S.No.	Plant species	Local name	Iron (mg/ 100g)	Copper (mg/ 100g)	Manganese (mg/ 100g)	Zn (mg/ 100g)
1.	*Amaranthus spinous*	Chauli	65.6	4.8	0.2	4.0
2.	*Basella rubra*	Poi	35.6	3.5	5.0	4.7
3.	*Brassica campestris*	Sarson	53.8	3.6	0.6	38.0
4.	*Brassica oleracea*	Phool Gobhi leaves	29.0	0.5	0.5	4.2
5.	*Chenopodium album*	Bathua	37.0	11.2	0.2	17.0
6.	*Colocasia esculantum*	Arbi	34.8	11.8	0.4	11.0
7.	*Cicer arietinum*	Channa sag	26.9	2.8	0.7	7.2
8.	*Ipomea aquticafrask*	Nari, Kalmi, Karemua	29.0	2.4	0.5	3.7
9.	*Moringa oleifera*	Sahjan leaves	20.6	2.0	0.2	5.3
10.	*Spinacia oleracea*	Palak	40.0	6.0	0.3	11.8
		Mean	37.32	4.86	0.86	10.69
		SD	13.38	3.81	1.47	10.54
		't' value	8.818	4.035	1.856	3.207

Nutritional Composition of Underutilized Leaves

Nutritional composition of underutilized leaves samples belonging to various families are shown in Table 5.27. These

Table 5.28. Micro nutrient content of underutilized leaves on dry weight basis

S.No.	Plant species	Local name	Protein (g)	Fat (g)	Calcium (mg)	β-carotene
1.	*Amaranthus spinous*	Chauli	3.0*	0.3*	800*	3.564*
2.	*Basella rubra*	Poi	13.33**	6.30**	202.9***	5606.6***
3.	*Brassica campestris*	Sarson	4.0*	0.6*	34*	2.622*
4.	*Brassica oleracea*	Phool Gobhi leaves	5.9*	1.3*	340*	230*
5.	*Chenopodium album*	Bathua	3.7*	0.4*	150*	1,5740*
6.	*Colocasia esculantum*	Arbi	13.7*	5.9*	—	15,700*
7.	*Cicer arietinum*	Channa sag	24.33**	4.03**	—	—
8.	*Ipomea aquticafrask*	Nari, Kalmi, Karemua	2.9*	0.4*	34*	1,980*
9.	*Moringa oleifera*	Sahjan leaves	6.7*	-	6,780*	—
10.	*Spinacia oleracea*	Palak	2.0*	0.7*	190*	9,440*

* = Nutritive value of Indian food (1999)

* = Pandey, V.N. and Srivastava, A.K. (1997).

* = Kumar *et al.* (1991)

\- = Not available

all values were not determined but reported on the basis of various researches carried out by different workers.

Protein content in leaves ranges from 2.0 g/100 g to 24.33 g/100 g in *Cicer arietinum.* Fat and lipid content ranges from 0.3 g to 5.9 g/100 in *Colocasia esculantum.* Calcium content ranges from 29 mg to 350 mg/100 g in cauliflower green (*Brassica oleracea* var. botrytis).

β-carotene values was found to be 240 μg to 15,700 μg in *Colocasia esculantum* followed by 9,440 μg in *Spinacia oleracea* and 5606.6 μg in *Basella rubra.*

Correlation between Different Variables

Significant correlation amongst variables were found and are presented in Table 5.29, 5.30, 5.31 and 5.32.

Energy intake was highly significantly related to protein fat, calcium and iron ($r = 0.781, 0.744, 0.490$ and 0.340) at 1 per cent level of significance, significant relation show that more intake of energy will provide more amount of these nutrients.

Protein was highly significantly related with fat, iron and calcium ($r = 0.780, 0.674, 0.557$ and 0.344). Fat and carotene have significant relation ($r = 0.266$ and 0.354) at 1 per cent level of significance, it reveals that more the fat in diet more will be the absorption of carotene because carotene is fat soluble and necessary for absorption, fat is a carrier of fat soluble vitamins (Robinson, 1980).

Iron was significantly related with manganese and carotene ($r = 0.360$ and 0.249) at 1 per cent and 5 per cent level of significance, this significant relation showed that carotene which are abundantly found in green leafy vegetable are also rich in iron.

Iron intake has significant relation with education and number of abortion ($r = 0.585$ and 0.445) at 5 per cent and 1 per cent level of significance, relation between variable revealed that educated women take iron in adequate amount

Table 5.29. Correlation coefficient between nutrients (within urban)

	Energy	Protein	Fat	Iron	Calcium	Caro-tene	Copper	Manga-nese	Zinc
Energy	—	0.329*	0.144	0.256*	0.116	0.091	-0.095	0.093	0.154
Protein		—	0.344**	0.118	0.674**	0.136	-0.120	0.081	0.094
Fat			—	0.154	-0.149	0.256**	-0.005	-0.061	0.025
Iron				—	0.104	-0.168	-0.125	-0.360**	0.071
Calcium					—	-0.195	-0.135	0.040	-0.029
Carotene						—	0.169	0.008	0.105
Copper							—	0.201	0.275*
Manganese								—	0.461**
Zinc									—

Table 5.30. Correlation coefficient between different variables (rural)

	Energy	Protein	Fat	Iron	Calcium	Caro-tene	Copper	Manga-nese	Zinc
Energy	—	0.781**	0.744**	0.340**	0.490**	0.254*	0.154	0.335*	0.087
Protein		—	0.780**	0.430**	0.557**	0.071	0.128	0.034	-0.089
Fat			—	0.191	0.319	0.354*	0.084	-0.308	-0.01
Iron				—	0.220	0.249	-0.148	-0.247	-0.147
Calcium					—	0.268**	-0.007	-0.203	-0.046
Carotene						—	0.030	-0.0738	-0.030
Copper							—	0.356**	-0.348
Manganese								—	0.222
Zinc									—

* Significant at 5 per cent level; ** Significant at 1 per cent level

Table 5.31. Correlation coefficient between different variables (urban)

	Iron	Copper	Manga-nese	Zinc	Education	Parity	Number of abortion	Birth interval	Income/ Capita
Iron	—	0.125	0.360**	0.0715	0.585**	-0.228	0.445*	0.126	0.105
Copper		—	0.201	0.275	-0.132	-0.286	0.0363	-0.283	0.332*
Manganese			—	0.461*	0.095	0.115	-0.325	-0.277	-0.346
Zinc				—	0.155	-0.198	0.041	0.037	0.061
Education					—	0.270	0.213	0.129	0.059
Parity						—	-0.476**	0.158	0.228
Number of abortion							—	0.308	0.245
Birth interval								—	0.229
Income/ capita									—

* Significant at 5 per cent level
** Significant at 1 per cent level

Table 5.32. Correlation coefficient between different variables

	Iron	Copper	Manga-nese	Zinc	Education	Parity	Number of abortion	Birth interval	Income/ Capita
Iron	—	-0.148	-0.247	-0.147	-0.334	-0.129	-0.060	-0.252	-0.116
Copper		—	-0.356**	-0.348*	0.183	0.086	-0.268	0.197	0.116
Manganese			—	0.222	0.022	0.083	0.198	-0.016	0.138
Zinc				—	-0.135	-0.054	-0.056	0.066	0.017
Education					—	-0.348	0.181	0.496**	0.427*
Parity						—	0.285	0.237	0.150
Number of abortion							—	-0.092	0.036
Birth interval								—	0.036
Income/ capita									—

* Significant at 5 per cent level
** Significant at 1 per cent level

and when iron intake is satisfactory there will be less chances of abortion.

Significant relation was also found in energy intake and manganese ($r = 0.335$) at 1 per cent level of significance and relation revealed that manganese play vital role in energy metabolism.

Education, birth interval and income/capita ($r = 0.496$ and 0.427) were significantly related at 1 per cent level of significance, relation showed that where there is more education, more opportunity of earning money through different sources are possible.

Negative significant correlation was found between copper and ($r = -0.356$ and -0.348 at 1% level of significance) zinc and manganese. This negative relation suggest that if copper content was more in green leafy vegetable it will inhibit the absorption of zinc and manganese, these element has antagonist relationship between each other and inhibit absorption by reducing bio-availability.

There was no correlation found between income per capita, number of abortion birth order.

6

CHAPTER

Summary and Conclusion

Adequate nutrition before and during pregnancy has greater potential for a long term health impact than it does at any other time. Maternal health is a complex, influenced by various genetic social and economic factors, infections and environmental conditions, many of which may affect the foetal growth. Physiological adaptations result in improved utilisation of nutrients either through increased absorption, decreased excretion or alternations in metabolism.

A woman who has been well nourished before conception begins her pregnancy with reserves of several nutrients so that the needs of the growing foetus can be met without affecting her health. Infants who are well nourished in the womb, have an enhanced chance of entering life in good physical and mental health. The effects of under-nutrition during reproduction will vary depending upon the nutrients involved, the length of time it is lacking and the stage of gestation at which it occurs.

A woman whose diet is adequate before pregnancy is usually able to bear a full term viable infant, without extensive modifications of her diet. Mother's diet should produce adequate nutrients so that maternal stores do not get depleted and produce sufficient milk to nourish her child after birth. The nutritional demands are highly increased in an adolescent mother.

Objectives

1. To study the socio-economic status of pregnant women.
2. To assess the clinical and Anthropometric measurement of pregnant women.
3. To assess the dietary pattern of pregnant women using food frequency and 24 hour call method.
4. To identify underutilized foods being consumed by local people of U.P.
5. To assess the micronutrients content, Fe, Cu, Mg and Zinc in identified underutilized food.

Research Methodology

The study was conducted in Farrukhabad district. Two blocks and ten localities were selected in this study. Total 220 pregnant women were selected. Dependent and independent variables were used such as age, caste, education, clinical survey, micro nutrient etc. The statistical tools were used such as S.D., arithmetic mean, t test, chi-square test etc.

Major Findings

1. 59.1 per cent rural pregnant women were belonged to 18 to 26 years age group while 45.5 per cent urban women have same age group. 29.1 per cent rural women have belonged to 26 to 34 years age group whereas 38.2 per cent urban women have belonged to same age group.
2. 52.7 per cent rural women and 43.6 per cent urban women were belonged to middle caste while 25.5 per cent rural women and 20.9 per cent urban pregnant

women have belonged to lower caste (SC/ST). 21.8 per cent rural women and 35.5 per cent urban women were of upper caste.

3. 47.3 per cent rural pregnant women were belonged to nuclear family and 52.7 per cent rural women have belonged to joint family system. 60.0 per cent urban women have belonged to nuclear family system while 40.0 per cent women in joint family system.
4. 29.2 per cent rural women have passed secondary level education, whereas 25.5 per cent urban women have passed graduate level education. 3.6 per cent rural women have educated up to post-graduate level whereas, 16.4 per cent urban women have educated up to post graduate level. 16.4 per cent rural women were educated up to intermediate whereas, 14.5 per cent urban women have educated up to intermediate. Education wise urban pregnant women were found more educated in comparison to rural pregnant women.
5. 28.2 per cent rural women are landless labourers. 21.8 per cent rural women were doing work according to caste occupation like growing vegetables, growing flowers while 22.7 per cent urban women were involved in caste occupation like selling vegetables, selling flowers and washing cloths. 12.7 per cent women (rural) were housewives while 39.2 per cent urban women have housewives.
6. 38.2 per cent rural and 50.9 per cent urban women were from whose monthly family income ₹ 10,000 to ₹ 15,000. 35.5 per cent rural and 15.5 per cent urban pregnant women were from whose monthly family income ₹ 5,000 to ₹ 10,000 10.9 per cent rural and 15.5 per cent urban pregnant women were from whose monthly family income ₹ 15,000 to ₹ 20,000.

7. 36.4 per cent rural pregnant women were lived in pucca and mixed house respectively, whereas 70.9 per cent urban pregnant women have pucca house. In rural area, 27.2 per cent women have kachcha house while 7.3 per cent urban women have kachcha house.
8. 83.6 per cent rural and 56.4 per cent urban pregnant women have no membership in any organization. 27.3 per cent urban and 16.4 per cent rural women were member in one organization.
9. 70.0 per cent rural and 94.5 per cent urban pregnant women have chair and table. Only 17.3 per cent rural and 41.8 per cent urban pregnant women possessed sofa set. Majority of both groups were having electric fan, transistor, television and two wheeler. In urban class most of the respondents have cooking gas, refrigerator, steel almirrah, electric iron and tape recorder.
10. There is general agreement that a relationship exists between maternal height and mean birth weight. Adequate nutrition before and during pregnancy has greater potential for a long term health impact than it does at any other time. Maternal health is a complex influenced by various genetic social and economic factors and environmental conditions many of which may affect the foetal growth.
11. Maternal nutrition factors such as low caloric intake or gestational weight gain, pre-pregnant weight, and height were the most important established determinants of intrauterine growth retardation (IUGR), LBW, perinatal, neonatal and infant mortality and poor infant growth.

    For optimal introutering growth and survival weight gain should be on an average around 9 kg. Both excess or low weight gain are associated with high incidence of prematurity, LBW and perinatal mortality.

Undernourished women gain 6.5 to 7 kg during pregnancy. Weight gain below 6 kg is associated with more than 55 per cent of the LBW babies. Adolescent mother require more nutrients than mature women to produce similar size infants, as her own nutrient requirements complete with those of her foetus.

12. BMI of pregnant women have increased according to age group. 27.0+1.6 BMI of rural women and 29.0+1.9 BMI of urban pregnant women were belonged to 34 to 42 years age group. The correlation coefficient between BMI of urban women and her age group was significant thus according to age group BMI was increased in urban area. Maternal nutritional status, both prior to and during pregnancy is a critical determinant of pregnancy outcomes, a positive and significant relationship between maternal pre-pregnancy weight for height and fetal size has been observed in both well-nourished and poorly nourished populations.

13. 44.5 per cent rural pregnant women and 29.1 per cent urban women were reported unwell in terms of nausea and 20.9 per cent rural and 12.7 per cent urban women was found to be ill, at complete bed rest.

    Hair examination indicate that 40.0 per cent rural and 49.1 per cent urban women having normal hair, 17.3 per cent rural and 26.4 per cent urban having thin and sparse hair.

    Lusterless hair and thin and sparse hair might be due to deficiency of protein in the diet.

    Clinical symptoms observed related to vision include xerosis, bitot spot, brown dipigmentation and pale eyes in cornea and conjunctiva both.

14. 95 (43.2%) pregnant women found to be had no miscarriage case. 66 (30.0%) women had at least one miscarriage and only 1 women was found to had more

than 8 times miscarriage. The exact reasons was not known for miscarriage. It was found that parity number and number of miscarriage have significant correlation.

15. 66.4 per cent rural women have vegetarian whereas 47.3 per cent urban pregnant women were taking vegetarian food in her meals. 52.7 per cent urban pregnant women were non-vegetarian whereas 33.6 per cent rural women have non-vegetarian. In comparison to rural women, urban women have taking more non-veg food in meals.
16. Average cereals 42.1 g/day by vegetarian rural women and 271 g/day by urban vegetarian women were taking whereas 410 g/day non-veg rural women and 264 g/day non-veg urban women consumed respectively. Rural women were taking more cereals g/day in comparison to urban women. 106 g/day average GLVs by non-veg rural women and 69 g/day GLVs by non-veg urban women were taking but its deficit by standard value. In Uttar Pradesh mean intake of cereal is significantly less than of 446 g per day as found by ICMR (1989). In rural area, this amount is even less than average intake of urban people. Green leafy vegetable (GLVs) are rich source of iron, calcium, â carotene, vitamin C, riboflavin and folic acid. At least 50 g of green leafy vegetable should be consumed in one's diet. In the present study both areas consumption was less than the comparable amount of 100 g per day.
17. Pregnant women of rural area was found 3669+211 Kcal per day and 2301+196 Kcal was found in urban pregnant women, value as compared to RDA was 13.5 per cent more in rural area and 8.9 per cent less in urban area.

    According to expert group of planning commission, nutritional norm per capita daily intake of 2400 Kcal in urban area population were come in below poverty line. So on the basis of this both area population were come in below poverty line. The major source of energy for both group (rural and urban) was cereal.

18. The caloric requirements of a pregnant women were mostly increased in the latter half of pregnancy in 2nd trimester required 90 cals/day and 3rd trimester 200 cals/day. The normal protein requirement of an adult women is 50 g/day and for pregnant women 65 g/day. For pregnant women the requirement of thiamin is increased by 0.2 mg/day.

19. 89.1 per cent urban women were taking cereals, 90.9 per cent urban women taking milk, 83.6 per cent urban women taking green vegetables, 87.3 per cent women taking fruit and 82.7 per cent urban women taking jaggery according to doctor advise. Majority of rural pregnant women have taking advise by elder women in family for special food. Less majority of rural women were taking advise of doctor for taking special food in diet.

    Dairy milk products are a primary source of calcium. Dried fruits, green leafy vegetables, eggs and enriched cereals and iron fertified salt product additional sources of iron. Milk, meat, egg and cheese are complete proteins and of high biological value. Additional protein may be obtained from legumes and whole grains, nuts and oilseeds.

20. 82.7 per cent rural pregnant women and 78.2 per cent urban pregnant women were avoiding papaya in the diet whereas 71.8 per cent rural women and 60.0 per cent urban women were not taking ginger in a diet. 69.1 per cent rural women and 74.5 per cent urban women were not taking tamarind while 84.5 per cent rural women and 54.5 per cent urban women were not taking high dose medicine during pregnancy period.

The birth of infant is the expectation of parents when pregnancy is considered. Normality is not limited to the time of birth, but includes the achievement of full potential in adulthood. Today advances in medical knowledge and delivery have made this aspiration more readily available than ever before.

Indeed modern technology poses a risk to the foetus and lactating infant from the drugs used in obstetric practice and from the increasing number of chemicals in the environment. New social cultural and ecologic conditions have modified the experience of today's pregnant women. Studies are needed to clarify their specific impact and facilitate the development of preventive and/or curative strategies.

21. 86.4 per cent urban pregnant women were faced nausea and vomiting may be due to nervous disturbances, placental protein intoxication or due to derangement in carbohydrate metabolism. Condition develop to hyperemesis gravidarum, a severe prolonged persistent vomiting, peripheral parenteral nutrition. 49.1 per cent rural women and 77.3 per cent urban pregnant women have faced constipation, the pressure of the enlarging uterus on the lower portion of the intestine in addition to the hormonal muscle relaxant effect of placental hormones on the gastrointestinal tract and physical inactivity may make elimination difficult.

    77.3 per cent rural women and 87.3 per cent urban women have suffered weight gain during pregnancy, optimal weight gain is about 11 to 13 kg about 900 to 1800 g is an average gain during the first trimester. Sharp sudden increase in weight after the 20th week of pregnancy. Excessive weight gain places an extra strain on the organs and increases the incidence to toxaemia.

Nausea in pregnancy may be due to nervous disturbances, placental protein intoxication or due to derangement in carbohydrate metabolism.

22. 69.1 per cent urban women have faced hypertensive disorders. Urinary tract infection and vaginal bleeding in pregnancy have in both side of women (rural and urban) during pregnancy.

    Physiological changes in the blood occur progressively during normal pregnancy. Haemoglobin mass increases, red blood cell volume increases, plasma volume rises and haemoglobin concentration drops from 13.4 to 11.6 g per 100 ml. Severe anaemia in pregnant women increases maternal morbidity and mortality and involves a higher risk of the foetus. A pregnant woman is labeled anaemic if from the 28th week onwards the haemoglobin is less than 10 g per 100 ml of blood.

23. Fruits were consume more in once a day and one per day 70.0 per cent urban pregnant women and 90.0 per cent rural pregnant women were consumed 1-2 times month and 1 to 2 times per week. 40 per cent rural pregnant women consume root and tuber once/day and 17.0 per cent urban women consume root tuber and other once/day. 35.0 per cent rural women were consume nuts and oilseed once a day whereas 37.3 per cent urban women were consume nuts and oilseeds.

24. 71.4 per cent to 96.6 per cent maximum in *Basella rubra* followed by 93.3 per cent in *Chenopodium album,* 90.9 per cent in *Ipomea aqutica,* 90.2 per cent in *Brassica campestris* on fresh weight basis. 88.2 per cent moisture in *Spinacia oleracea* and 77.8 per cent moisture in Channa sag.

25. Protein content in leaves ranges from 2.0 g/100 g to 24.33 g/100 g in *Cicer arietinum.* Fat and lipid content

ranges from 0.3 g to 5.9 g/100 in *Colocasia esculantum.* Calcium content ranges from 29 mg to 350 mg/100 g in cauliflower green (*Brassica oleracea* var. botrytis).

β-carotene values was found to be 240 µg to 15,700 µg in *Colocasia esculantum* followed by 9,440 ìg in *Spinacia oleracea* and 5606.6 µg in *Basella rubra.*

26. Protein was highly significantly related with fat, iron and calcium (r = 0.780, 0.674, 0.557 and 0.344). Fat and carotene have significant relation (r = 0.266 and 0.354) at 1 per cent level of significance, it reveals that more the fat in diet more will be the absorption of carotene because carotene is fat soluble and necessary for absorption, fat is a carrier of fat soluble vitamins.

Iron was significantly related with manganese and carotene (r = 0.360 and 0.249) at 1 per cent and 5 per cent level of significance, this significant relation showed that carotene which are abundantly found in green leafy vegetable are also rich in iron.

Suggestions, Recommendation and Policy Implications

1. Routine provision of a daily supplement throughout pregnancy would significantly decrease the number of mother are clearly vitamin D deficient, reducing related serious risks to their babies.
2. Taking vitamin D supplements during pregnancy is not only safe for mother and baby but it can also prevent preterm labour births and infections.
3. Taking a multivitamins pills during pregnancy can dramatically cut the chances of having an underweight baby.
4. There is need to update information on the content of micronutrient in locally available low cost leafy vegetable using modern procedure. And there is also

need to identify optimal ways of using these foods singly or in combination for combating micronutrient malnutrition.

5. In order to achieve an improvement in the quality of the habitual diets in poor households, emphasis should be on food based rather than drug based or pharmaceutical short cuts so food resources available with in the country should be put to maximum use instead of restoring to commercial pharmaceutical short cuts.

Bibliography

Anderson, L.T. (2002). Food and Nutrient Intakes Among Pregnant Women in Rural Tamilnadu India. *Public Health Nutrition,* **6**(2) : 131-137.

Andrew Tomkins (2001). Nutrition and Maternal Morbidity and Mortality, *Br. J. Nutri.* **85**(2) : 593-99.

Azais, Braesco, V.; Pasca, G. (2000). Vitamin A in Pregnancy : Requirements and Safety Limits. *Am. J. Clin. Nutri.,* **71** (supp.), 1325-1333.

Beach, *et al.* (1982). Reversibility of Development Retardation following Murine Fatal Zinc Deprivation. *J. Nutri.,* **112** : 1169-1181.

Bharti, R. and Umamaheshwari *et al.* (2000). Use of Non-traditional Leafy Vegetable for Food Security, Food and Nutrition. News, April, ANGR Agriculture University, Hyderabad.

Black, E. Robert *et al.* (2001). Micronutrients in Pregnancy, *Br. Jr. Nutri,*(2001) **85**. supp. 2 : 5193-5197.

Chaudhari, S.N. (2002). International Life Science Institute, Vol. **60**, pp. 102-108(7). http://www.1.hSI.org.in.

Devi and Sarojini G. (2000). Food and Nutrient Intake, Deficiencies and KAP of Pregnant and Lactating Women Belonging to Dairy and Non-Dairy Families. *J. Res. ANGRAU,* **28**(1 and 2) : 65-68.

Gautan, V.P. *et al.* (2002). Dietary Aspects of Pregnant Women in Rural Areas of Northern India. http://www.virtual.addition.com.

Giddens *et al.* (2000). Mallnutrition Among Pregnant Women. pp. 102-104. http://www.DFN.org.in.

Godfrey, K. and Robinsons, S. (1998). Maternal Nutrition Placental Growth and Fetal Programming. *Prec. Nutri. Soc.,* **57** : 105-111.

Goldenberg, *et al.* (1995). The Effect of Zinc Supplementation on Pregnancy outcome. *J. Am. Medi. Assoc.,* **274** : 463-468.

Gopalan, C. and Patnaik, R. (2002). Essential Fatty Acids in Maternal and Infant Nutrition, *Indian J. Biochem. Biophy.,* **39** : 303-311.

Gopalan, C. *et al.* (2000). Multiple Micronutrient Supplementation in Pregnancy, http://www.nutrition foundation of India. Org/ archives/APR 2KB.HTN-29.k.

Gopalan, *et al.* (2000). Multiple Micronutrient Supplementation in Pregnancy, http://www.nutrition foundation of India.org./ ARCHIVES/APR2KB. H.T.M-29K.

Griffiths, P.L. (2001). The Nutrition Transition is Underway in India. *Journal of Nutrition*, **131**(10) : 2692-2700.

Guirindala, O. Mildred (2006). http://www.ifpri/focus/05-07 htm.

Gupta (1999). Attaining Global Health : Challenges and Opportunities. Population Bulletin of the Population, **55**(1) : 3-48. www.cicred.org.in.

Gupta, Prabha, S. (1999). Nutrition an Indian Prospecline. *Ind. J. Pub. Health* (1) : 11-16.

Hininger, I. *et al.* (2002). Controlled Trial in Opportunity Healthy Pregnant Women. http://www.IFRI.org.in.

International Journal of *Food Science and Nutrition* (1998). Vol. **49**, pp. 243-247.

Ireno, Kalm (2009). Nutritional Status of Pregnant Women and Birth Outcome. *Jr. of Przeglad lekarski.* http://www.researchgate.net/ publication/26768545 Nutritional status of pregnant women.

Jaydev, J. (2002). Nutritional Security for All, *Yojana,* September, pp. 35-36.

Joseph, O. (2009). Food Aversion and Craving Among Pregnant Women in Akure, *International Jr. of Tropical Medicine,* **4**(3) : 100-103, http:// www. Medwelljournals.com./fullltexlt/ijtm/2009/100-103.pdf.

King, J.C. (2000). Physiology of Pregnancy and Nutrient Metabolism. *Medi.J. Clm. Nutri.,* **71** : 1218-1255.

Kumar, *et al.* (1999). Nutritional status of Women and Children in West Bengal, Challenges and Opportunities, *Indian J. Pub. Health,* **43** : 1, 1720.

Lomborg (2004). Global Crises, Global Solutions Cambridge. Cambridge University Press.

Madeleine, H. (2008). Malnutrition in Middle Class Pregnant Women. http://www.britannica.com/eobi/article?

Mathuravali, S.M.D.; Manimegalai, S.N. and Jayalakshmi (2001). Effect of Socio-economic Status on Nutritional Status of Pregnant Women and Pregnancy Outcome in Selected Urban Slum of Madurai Districts. *Indian J. Nutri. Dietet.,* **38**(10) : 350-357.

Mc. Phail, P. and Bothwell, T.H. (1992). The Prevalence and Cause of Nutritional Iron Deficiency. In : Nutritional Anaemias : Fomon 2 (ed) Raven Press, New York, pp. 1-3.

Monteiro *et al.* (2002). Obesity in Latin American Women and Children. *J. Nutrition,* **28**(9) : 1469-1473.

Monteiro *et al.*(2002). Socio-economic Status and Obesity in Adult Populations of Developing Countries. A Review Bulletin of World Health Organization, **82**(12) : 940-946.

Mundra, A. and Mathur *et al.* (2000). Effect of Supplementation of Leaf Concentrate on Haemoglobin and Blood Profiles of Adolescent Girls. *J. Fd. Sci. Teach.,* **27**(6) : 617-619.

Nuccia, B.L. *et al.* (2001). Nutritional Status of Pregnant Women : Prevalence and Associated Pregnancy Outcome. http://www.gestaoerh.com.br/artigos/ log.

Osendarp *et al.* (2000). A Randomized, Placebo Controlled Trial of the Effect of Zinc Supplementation During Pregnancy on Pregnancy Outcome in Bangladeshi Urban Poor. *Am. J. Clin. Nutri.,* **71** : 114-119.

Radhakrishna *et al.* (2004). Malnutrition Among Women in Kerala. An Analysis of Trends, Differentials and Determinants Communication Division, World Food Programme. www.wfp.org.

Raj Kamla (2008). Stud. Home Comm. Sci. **2**(1) : 7-10.

Ratzan *et al.* (2000). Food and Agriculture Organisation. Food and Nutrition Paper No. 56, Rome, FAO.

Rouse (2003). Potential Cost Effectiveness of Nutrition Interventions to Prevent Adverse Pregnancy Outcomes in the Developing World. *Journal of Nutrition,* 133.

Sachan Alok *et al.* (2005). High Prevalence of Vitamin D Deficiency Among Pregnant Women in Northern India. http://www.PGI/INDE.in.

Sachdev, H.P.S. *et al.* (1997). Nutritional Status of Women and Children in India, http://www.nutrition foundation of India.org.

Scholl, T.O. and Johnson *et al.* (2000). Folic Acid Influence on the Outcome of Pregnancy. *Am. J. Clin. Nutri.,* **71** : 1295-1303.

Shinha (2009). http://pdfcast.org/pdf/studies-on-the-predisposing-factors-of-protein-energy-malnutrition-lamong-pregnant-women-ion-a-nigerian-community.

Singh, S. and Singh, R. (1997). Nutritional and Obstetric Outcome of Rural Pregnant Punjabi Women as Influenced by Nutrition Counselling. *J. Res. P.A.U.,* **34**(3) : 344-353.

Sudesh Jood *et al.* (2002). *Journal of Nutrition and Health* Vol. **16**, pp. 121-131(23) ref.

Umamaheshwari, *et al.* (1997). Maternal Malnutrition and Pregnancy Outcome. In Recent Advances in Nutrition for Vulnerable groups.

Umamaheswari, *et al.* (1997). Maternal Malnutrition and Pregnancy Outcome. In Recent Advances in Nutrition for Vulnerable Groups.

Umamaheswari, K. (1997). Maternal Malnutrition and Pregnancy Outcome. In Recent Advances in Nutrition for Vulnerable Groups.

UNICEF (1997). Nutrition Translation in India. *Publ. Health Nutrition*, **5**(1A) : 175-182.

UNICEF (2007). Dietary Advice During Pregnancy, pp. 12-14.

Uthman, O.A. and Aremu, O. (2007). http://www.rrh.org.au.

Vazir, S. (1999). Malnutrition and Psychological Development in Textbook of Human Nutrition. Oxford and IBH Publ. Co. Pvt. Ltd., New Delhi.

Wellinghausen, N. Martin and Rink, L. (1997). Zinc Inhibits Interleukin 1. Dependent T-cell Stimulation, *European J. Immuno*, **27** : 2529-2535.

West *et al.* (1999). Double Blind, Cluster Randomized Trial of Low Dose Supplementation with Vitamin A or Beta Carotene on Mortality Related Pregnancy in Nepal. The NNIPS-2 study group Br. Med. J., **318** : 570-575.

WHO (1992). The Prevalence of Anaemia in Women : A Tabulation of Available Information Maternal Health and Safe Motherhood and Nutrition Programme, Geneva.

WHO (1997). Obesity Epidemic Puts Millions at Risk From Related Disease. WHO Press Release 46, June 19, http://www.WHO.org.in.

Zulfiqar *et al.* (2004). Maternal and Child Health. In South Asia Ready for Change. BMJ, 328.

Valeri (2010). "Gestational and Malnutrition Related Diabetes". 23 July, 2010. http://easyonlinejob'sreview.com/

Haghdoost Ali-Akbar (2010) "Prevalence of Iron Deficiency Anaemia Among Iranian Pregnant Women". 24 Feb. 2010. http://www.thefreelibrary.com/

Ians (2010). "Pregnant Women Should Be Given Vitamin D Supplements". 4th July, 2010. http://blog.taragana.com/

Ians (2010). "Excessive Calcium Can Cause Harm". 2nd June 2010. http://blog.taragana.com/

Ians (2010). "Vitamin D Supplements Can Prevent Premature Birth" 1st May, 2010. http://blog.taragana.com/

Ians (2010). "Large Dose of Vitamin D in Pregnancy Cuts Premature Birth". 1st May, 2010. http://blog.taragana.com/

Ani (2010). "Taking Multivitamins' Cuts Chances of Having an Underweight – baby". 23rd April, 2010. http://blog.taragana.com/

Ani (2010). "Vitamin C and E Supplements Don't Cut Risk for BP Disorders of Pregnancy". 8th April, 2010. http://blog.taragana.com

Index